THE LAST RIDE OF THE JAMES–YOUNGER GANG

Jesse James and the Northfield Raid 1876

SEAN McLACHLAN

First published in Great Britain in 2012 by Osprey Publishing, Midland House, West Way, Botley, Oxford, OX2 0PH, UK 44-02 23rd Street, Suite 219, Long Island City, NY 11101, USA E-mail: info@ospreypublishing.com

Osprey Publishing is part of the Osprey Group

A CIP catalog record for this book is available from the British Library

Print ISBN: 978 1 84908 599 1
PDF ebook ISBN: 978 1 84908 600 4
ePub ebook ISBN: 978 1 78200 308 3

Index by Zoe Ross
Typeset in Sabon
Map by bounford.com
Battlescenes and BEVs by Peter Dennis
Originated by PDQ Digital Media Solutions, Bungay, UK

Printed in China through Worldprint Ltd.

12 13 14 15 16   10 9 8 7 6 5 4 3 2 1

Osprey Publishing is supporting the Woodland Trust, the UK's leading woodland conservation charity, by funding the dedication of trees.

www.ospreypublishing.com

DEDICATION

To my wife, Almudena, and my son, Julián

ACKNOWLEDGMENTS

Numerous researchers helped with the preparation of this book. I'd like to thank the staff at the Northfield Historical Society and the Missouri State Archives for digging into their files for rare photographs. Specialists at the Missouri in the Civil War Message Board and Jesse James Discussion Site pointed the way to several good leads. I'd also like to thank researcher Shawn Douglas of St. Louis for his tireless efforts in finding obscure facts about 19th-century trains, and to Missouri historian Larry Wood for some timely information about the bandit Hobbs Kerry.

A NOTE TO THE READER

As anyone working in law enforcement will attest, most people make terrible witnesses. The events at Northfield were recorded in numerous letters, diaries, newspaper reports, and official documents. It seems that everyone who was there – and many who weren't – wanted to tell their part in the drama. Then, as now, newspaper reporters weren't averse to making things up in order to make the story sound better or to fill in blanks. The only robber to give a detailed account of the events was Cole Younger, who actually gave several versions of his story and whose autobiography shows plenty of evidence that the lily was gilded quite heavily. Thus the accounts of that day are often contradictory. In this book we have chosen the majority opinions and assembled a consistent narrative from them. Important variants are also mentioned. Those interested in the many other twists to this tale are referred to the bibliography.

PHOTOGRAPHS

All photos credited (LoC) are courtesy the Library of Congress, Prints and Photographs Division. (Title page image) A bandit entertains the crowd at Northfield's annual "Defeat of Jesse James Days." (Northfield Historical Society)

ARTIST'S NOTE

Readers may care to note that the original paintings from which the color plates in this book were prepared are available for private sale. All reproduction copyright whatsoever is retained by the Publishers. All inquiries should be addressed to:

Peter Dennis, "Fieldhead," The Park, Mansfield, Nottinghamshire NG18 2AT, UK, or email magie.h@ntlworld.com

The Publishers regret that they can enter into no correspondence upon this matter.

CONTENTS

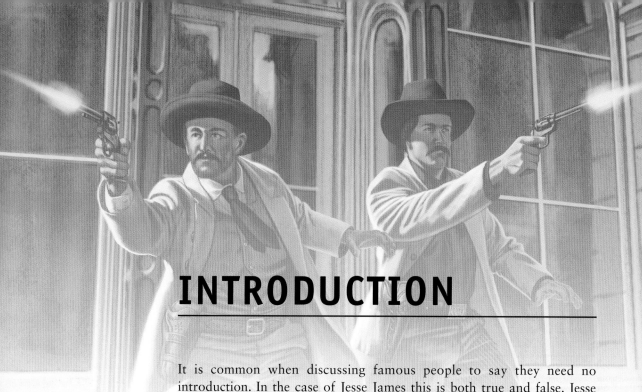

INTRODUCTION

It is common when discussing famous people to say they need no introduction. In the case of Jesse James this is both true and false. Jesse James is the most famous outlaw in history, but most of what the public "knows" about him is fable. Here is a brief overview of his life, along with the life of his older brother and fellow outlaw, Frank.

Frank and Jesse James were born in 1843 and 1847, respectively, on a farm near Kearney, western Missouri. Their father was a preacher who left for California's gold fields while they were still children and died there. Their mother, Zerelda, a strong frontier woman, raised them on her own, with only minimal help from her second and third husbands. The third was the mild-mannered Dr. Reuben Samuel, who, while never quite a father figure to the boys, was loved by them.

Western Missouri in the mid- to late 1850s was a region at war. The question of whether the neighboring territory of Kansas would become a free or slave state led to violent action from the opposing factions. Missourians crossed the border en masse to rig territorial elections. This was eventually stopped, but the conflict grew ever more violent. Free-State guerrillas called Jayhawkers raided Missouri, killing slave owners and bringing their slaves back to Kansas and freedom. Missouri bushwhackers crossed the state line, killed Free-Staters, and destroyed abolitionist newspaper offices. The war between Jayhawkers and bushwhackers was the first chapter in the American Civil War and one of the main factors that led to the larger war. While the James family, being slave owners living close to the border, were lucky they didn't lose their property, they certainly knew people who suffered.

Once the war started in earnest in 1861, Frank was quick to enlist, joining the rebellious Missouri State Guard that May. He saw action at the Confederate victory at Wilson's Creek on August 10 and again during the successful siege of Lexington, Missouri, from September 11 to 20. The State Guard was then forced to retreat in the face of a superior Union force back

Jesse James as a teenaged Confederate guerrilla or "bushwhacker" in Missouri. This picture, taken July 10, 1864, shows him wearing a loose "guerrilla shirt" and wielding three Colt Navy revolvers, a favorite weapon among the bushwhackers and used by many outlaws after the war. This image is reversed and has led to the persistent misunderstanding that Jesse was left-handed. He was, in fact, right-handed. The photo was taken in Platte City, Missouri, when Jesse and other guerrillas raided the town to support a mutiny of the local Union militia. Three hundred militiamen changed sides and raised a rebel flag. (LoC)

to southwestern Missouri. Along the way Frank fell ill, got left behind, and was captured and paroled. In return for swearing not to take up arms against the Union, he was allowed to return home. He might have farmed peacefully for the rest of the war if it were not for General Order No. 19, enacted in July of 1862, which forced all able-bodied men, including paroled Confederates, to join local Union militias. Frank, like many others, couldn't bring himself to don a Union uniform and fled. He joined the guerrilla band of William Quantrill.

Quantrill's band was making a name for itself with its lightning hit-and-run tactics, ability to elude pursuit, aggressive fighting style, and its ill-treatment of Unionist civilians. To join, one had to show ability with a gun and horse and answer "yes" to the following questions, "Will you follow orders, be true to your fellows, and kill all those who serve and support the Union?"

The Lawrence Massacre of August 21, 1863 by Quantrill's group of bushwhackers was the worst atrocity against civilians in the war. The band descended on abolitionist Kansas, gunned down nearly 200 mostly unarmed men and boys, and burned the town. Frank James and Cole Younger were there that day, but showed little remorse in later years. (LoC)

It soon became known that the James family farm was a rest area for Quantrill's guerrillas. The local militia (the same one Frank was supposed to have joined) showed up at the farm and demanded to know where Frank and his friends were. The soldiers beat Jesse, who was only 15, and tied a rope around his stepfather's neck. They then hauled Reuben Samuel up, let him drop, then hauled him up again. Eventually he broke and revealed Frank's hiding place. A brief skirmish ensued but the guerrillas got away. Samuel is believed to have suffered permanent brain damage as a result of his near hanging.

This incident instilled in Frank and Jesse a burning hatred of the North. Jesse was still too young to join the guerrillas, however, and they were probably not impressed when he shot the tip of his finger off while reloading a pistol. Being a good Baptist boy, he didn't swear even under these trying circumstances and instead shouted out, "Dingus!" Dingus became his nickname for the rest of his life.

Meanwhile Frank was getting his revenge. Quantrill's band rode roughshod over the region, raiding Lawrence, Kansas, on August 21, 1863, where they killed almost 200 mostly unarmed men and boys and torched the town. Frank was there that day, as was future outlaw Cole Younger. The massacre shocked both North and South and even some of the guerrillas didn't like Quantrill's methods. The band broke up that winter, some thinking Quantrill was too bloodthirsty and others thinking he was too much of a disciplinarian. These latter coalesced around Quantrill's lieutenant,

Bloody Bill Anderson. Frank went with Anderson, and Jesse, now 16, joined him in the spring of 1864.

Memories of the massacre lingered with Cole Younger. He joined the Christian Church on August 21, 1913, the 50th anniversary of the massacre. Explaining his actions long after the war he said:

> My father was opposed to the war and had friends on both sides but was shot down in cold blood and robbed by a gang of federal freebooters as he was driving home from Kansas City. That day changed my whole life. The knowledge that my father had been killed in cold blood filled my heart with lust for vengeance.

This statement is only partially true. Cole had, in fact, joined the guerrillas before his father was killed by Union troops. This is only one of the many instances where publicity-hungry Cole tried to make himself look better for the press.

Jesse was shot through the lung that summer while trying to steal a saddle from a civilian. He recovered under the care of his cousin Zerelda. The two soon fell in love and he started calling her "Zee" so as not to have to use the same name as his mother. Within a month or two he was back in the saddle, in time to take part in Anderson's bloody raid through central Missouri in support of a Confederate invasion led by General Sterling Price. Price moved up from Arkansas with 12,000 men in an ill-fated attempt to take St. Louis. Anderson's raid left scores dead, including many civilians and unarmed Union soldiers, but Price's invasion was repulsed.

As Price's mangled army staggered back to Arkansas, Bloody Bill was killed by a plucky Union militia. Riding with him that day was future James–Younger gang member Clell Miller. He was only 14 at the time and was captured in the skirmish. Miller claimed he had been kidnapped by Anderson's men and had only been with them for three days. This has been questioned by historians, but the support of several prominent neighbors and his tender age secured his release.

At this point Frank and Jesse rejoined Quantrill. The guerrilla leader decided to lead his men to Kentucky to continue the fight; he even claimed he wanted to ride to the capital and assassinate Lincoln. Jesse, perhaps seeing the war was coming to an end, decided not to follow and remained in Missouri with some other guerrillas. Frank did follow, as did future outlaw Jim Younger, brother of Cole. Quantrill's group was dogged by Union detachments. In one skirmish Jim Younger was captured but later escaped. On May 10, 1865 Quantrill's band was run to ground by Unionist guerrillas as fierce as themselves. Quantrill was mortally wounded and at least two of his followers were killed. Frank James was

Gen. Sterling Price led Missouri Confederate forces on numerous campaigns. Guerrillas such as the James and Younger brothers supported his actions behind Union lines. (LoC)

These bushwhackers from Quantrill's group were Frank James' and Cole Younger's comrades-in-arms. Dave Poole, is shown standing, and seated are Arch Clements (left) and Bill Hendricks (right). The photo was taken while they were wintering in Texas. They didn't like the image and trashed the photographer's equipment. Clements rode with the James–Younger gang in their first heist, the Liberty bank robbery. He was gunned down later that year by the state militia while resisting arrest. (LoC)

lucky to get away with his life. Seeing the war was now truly at an end, Frank gave up on July 26.

Jesse had been riding with the remnants of Anderson's old band in Missouri in the spring of 1865, but as the major Confederate armies laid down their arms, the hardcore bushwhackers began to give up hope. Some surrendered and found to their delight that they weren't lynched. Others fled to the Far West. Jesse and a group of comrades tried to surrender at Lexington, Missouri, on May 15 and were fired upon by some jumpy Union soldiers. Jesse was shot through the same lung as before, and again nearly died. He formally surrendered on May 21. Again in the care of his family, he and Zee became secretly engaged.

Life for former Confederates was hard in Missouri. The state government banned them from voting, holding public office, or serving in several professions. Many returning Confederates, especially in the Ozark region, found their land had been taken from them for failure to pay taxes and was being now farmed by Unionists. Some ex-bushwhackers, unable to put the killing behind them, used this persecution as an excuse to turn to outlawry.

The first heist by the James–Younger gang was less than a year after the war, on February 13, 1866, when some ten to 13 men robbed the Clay County Savings Association Bank in Liberty, Missouri. It was owned by staunch Unionists, which made it more attractive to the former rebels than Liberty's other, politically neutral, bank. The robbers got about $57,000 in what was the first American daytime bank robbery in peacetime. It's unclear who made up the gang, but Cole Younger and Frank James are commonly believed to have been there. Despite popular tradition, Jesse probably wasn't, because he was still laid up with his gunshot wound.

It is commonly believed that Jesse was in charge of the gang. He was certainly better known, thanks to his letters to various newspapers proclaiming his innocence. The more daring and better looking of the brothers, it is he who has become a legend, but it might have been Frank who was really in charge. Gang member George Shepard told a newspaperman, "Frank is the most shrewd, cunning, and capable; in fact, Jesse can't compare with him. Frank is a man of education, and can act the fine gentleman on all occasions. Jesse is reckless, and a regular dare-devil in courage, but it's Frank who makes all the plans and perfects the methods of escape. Jesse is a fighter and that's all. Why, he can't hardly read or write, and these stories about his writing to the Kansas City papers and the *Nashville Banner* is all stuff. If any letters were ever written, *Frank wrote them.*" [16–17]

Shepard added that Frank didn't mind Jesse stealing the show because Frank, "would rather not be known, so he directs Jesse and Jesse directs the

THOMAS COLEMAN "COLE" YOUNGER (JANUARY 15, 1844– MARCH 21, 1916)

The oldest of the three outlaw Younger brothers, Cole grew up on a wealthy farm in western Missouri. He joined Quantrill's guerrillas shortly after the outbreak of the Civil War in 1861. While he claimed he joined to avenge the murder of his father at the hands of a Union militia, in fact he joined months before that, although the murder certainly gave him a lingering hatred of the North. He also claimed he was a captain under the famous Confederate cavalry raider Brigadier General J.O. Shelby, but other than Cole's own account, there is no evidence for this.

After the war, he helped found the James–Younger gang and participated in its first robbery, that of the Clay County Savings Association in Liberty, Missouri, in 1866. Cole went on to commit a series of robberies, both with the James brothers and independently with one or more of his brothers and other outlaws. While his main area of activity was Missouri, he may have participated in two bank robberies in Kentucky, another in West Virginia, a stagecoach robbery in Arkansas, and a train robbery in Iowa.

His age and greater wartime experience made him the dominant of the three brothers. Cole was said to have been level-headed, cool under fire, and didn't like the more showy and hot-headed Jesse James. Cole could be showy himself, though. After his capture at Hanska Slough, he gave numerous and often contradictory interviews about his life, often stating he was sorry about the robbery, trying to clear his name of many crimes, and justifying the Lawrence Massacre.

After serving a 25-year sentence, he held various jobs including selling tombstones, running a Wild West show with Frank James, and going on the lecture

Cole Younger was the most experienced of the outlaw Youngers and reportedly had doubts about the wisdom of the Northfield heist before, during, and certainly after the raid. Here he is shown shortly after his capture at Hanska Slough. The wound to his temple that knocked him out is clearly visible. (Northfield Historical Society)

circuit talking about how crime doesn't pay. In 1903 he wrote the book *The Story of Cole Younger by Himself: An Auto-biography of the Missouri Guerrilla, Confederate Cavalry Officer, and Western Outlaw*. It's a fascinating if unconvincing read. He is not known to have committed any crimes after his release.

crowd. He [Jesse] likes notoriety and always takes care to let the people on trains know that he is the leader, and he always enjoyed the reading of his exploits in the papers."

On October 30, another bank was robbed in Lexington, Missouri, although the four robbers only got a little more than $2,000. On May 23, 1867, a dozen men robbed a bank in Richmond, Missouri. The robbers bagged some $3,500 but had to shoot their way out and left the mayor, the local jailor, and jailor's son dead.

In the meantime Cole Younger had been developing a reputation as a robber with a string of heists to his name. He worked with both the James

The interior and the vault of the Clay County Savings Association, Liberty, Missouri – robbed by the James–Younger gang in their first heist. (Sean McLachlan)

gang and his own people. Both gangs had a fluid membership and were only the "James–Younger gang" on certain jobs.

Cole was born to a prosperous family near Lee's Summit in Jackson County, Missouri, on January 15, 1844. A large, muscular man, he stood six feet, four inches, which was considered quite tall in those days. He was bright and friendly, yet easily aroused to volcanic anger. One man who worked with him in his later circus years said, "During my years on the frontier, and later in the Oklahoma oil fields, I have known many men with a command of profanity – freighters, cattle drovers, muleskinners, bullwhackers, and pipeliners. But none could approach Cole Younger's brand of invective. Nor was there anything lacking in his personal courage."

Jesse James captured the public imagination with his ability to fight off the law. This struck a chord with many rural Americans and former secessionists who mistrusted lawmen and anyone who represented the government or moneyed interests. While many of the stories about him were true, many more were invented or adapted from tales of earlier outlaws such as Dick Turpin and Claude Duval to embellish his exploits. Jesse encouraged this by sometimes signing his letters to the press using these names. (LoC)

Like many former bushwhackers, Cole claimed that he was persecuted for his wartime activities. This seems to be an exaggeration, since the Youngers and Jameses at first lived openly at their family farms. The bushwhackers-turned-outlaws don't seem to have suffered any worse than anyone else. In fact, being relatively prosperous, the Younger and James families were better off than many Unionists in a state where both sides suffered from the devastation of war.

Whether Cole Younger really tried to live within the law after the war is a mystery. He was involved in a bank robbery just one year after the war, but in 1868, he and another man captured two horse thieves and brought them to jail in Independence. Jesse James also struggled with his conscience. In September of 1869, Jesse asked to have his name struck from the membership of Mount Olive Baptist Church "for the stated reason that he believed himself unworthy."

On December 7, 1869, the gang struck the bank at Gallatin, Missouri, killing a bank employee. The robbers bragged that they'd shot Samuel P. Cox, the militia commander whose unit had killed Bloody Bill Anderson. It turned out they got the wrong man, but this shows there was some political motive beyond just grabbing easy money. A horse left behind was traced to Jesse. The law converged on his family farm but the brothers shot their way out.

It was at this time that Jesse began his letter-writing campaign to the Missouri papers, especially the *Kansas City Times*, where John Newman Edwards was editor. Edwards had ridden with Confederate cavalry raider J.O. Shelby during the war and saw the young ex-bushwhacker as the perfect new hero for the unreconstructed South. More robberies followed, with the gang expanding into Iowa and Kentucky. Their greatest escapade was robbing the cashbox of the Kansas City Exposition on September 26, 1872.

Group picture of the Younger family. Clockwise from left: Robert Younger, Henrietta Younger, Cole Younger, and James Younger. Henrietta was one of the outlaws' sisters and worked as a schoolteacher. (LoC)

This was done in front of a huge crowd and this daring act, along with Edwards' glowing newspaper account of the robbery, did much to create their fame.

Their notoriety increased on January 3, 1874, when they robbed a train at Gads Hill, Missouri. This hamlet had only 15 citizens. Five members of the gang, all wearing hoods, rounded up the entire population and put them under guard while they robbed the only store. As the train approached, one outlaw flagged it down with a red flag. The train stopped, the gang pulled out their revolvers, and made off with about $4,000 from the express mail and a few hundred dollars from the passengers. The technique of rounding up the locals to keep them from causing trouble and using a red signal to get the train to make an emergency stop was a signature of the gang. It is thought that one or more of the Younger brothers rode with the James brothers on this heist because the outlaws fled to St. Clair County, where the Youngers often hid out.

The James–Younger gang was not the first to rob a train in peacetime. That dubious honor goes to the Reno gang of Indiana, whose first train heist was on October 6, 1866. Gads Hill was Missouri's first peacetime train robbery, however, and predictably made headlines across the state.

The Younger brothers – Cole, Jim, John, and Bob – were treated as prime suspects. John Younger was already wanted over the 1871 killing of a Dallas lawman who had been trying to arrest him over a shooting. Now two Pinkerton agents and their local guide went to the Youngers' neighborhood to track them down over the Gads Hill affair. They were bushwhacked by Jim and John Younger. John Younger, one of the Pinkertons, and the guide were all killed in the ensuing gunfight. Another Pinkerton tried to catch the James brothers by foolishly showing up at their farm posing as a laborer looking for work. His body was found by a road many miles away.

The James and Younger brothers moved around constantly, Jesse and Frank keeping in contact with their family by letters written in code. Despite the price on their heads, the Jameses often visited home, their frightened neighbors not daring to report them to authorities. On the night

The James farm and (below) the window through which the Pinkerton bomb was thrown. This attack, which killed Frank and Jesse's half-brother and maimed their mother, did much to bring national sympathy to the "James boys." (Sean McLachlan)

of January 25, 1875, a group of agents surrounded the James farm and threw a firebomb through one of the windows. It exploded, killing Archie Samuel, Frank's and Jesse's half-brother, and destroying their mother's hand. The James brothers were not at the farm that night, and the attack drew widespread condemnation against the Pinkertons and fueled the James legend even more. The Hannibal and Saint Joseph Railroad, which had transported the Pinkertons on a special train that night, gave Mrs. Samuel a free lifetime pass for her and her companions. It was never robbed by the gang.

ORIGINS

The origins of the Northfield raid go back to someone who at that time wasn't even a member of the James–Younger gang – Hobbs Kerry. A coal miner with dreams of riches, he became friends with three members of the gang's outer circle: the Younger brothers' half-uncle Bruce Younger, Charlie Pitts, and Bill Stiles. Pitts' real name was Sam Wells but his only claim to fame is what he did under his alias Charlie Pitts and that is how he is known to history. Pitts was a neighbor of the Youngers in Lee's Summit, and may have done some work with them before. Bill Stiles went under the name Bill Chadwell and several other aliases. He'd been involved in many crimes ranging from selling liquor to the Indians to stealing a bottle of perfume from a drug store. Stiles had done some time in jail for horse thievery.

In the spring of 1876, Hobbs Kerry decided to use these secondhand connections to gain fame and fortune. He proposed that they hit Granby, Missouri, where a bank in the rich zinc-and-lead mining region promised good takings. It's unclear how far planning went, but word leaked out and plainclothes policemen were soon prowling around the mining camps hoping to nip the robbery in the bud. They did; word of their investigation somehow got back to the robbers and they abandoned the plan.

Kerry, Pitts, and Stiles went in search of the Younger and James brothers, still wanting to be in the gang. Stiles may have met Jesse before this and convinced him of the possibilities of a bank heist in Minnesota. Frank James met them and, suspicious, pulled a gun on Stiles, saying he thought Stiles was a detective and that he had a notion to shoot him. Eventually he remembered the man and took the three to see Jesse and Cole. They soon met up with Bob Younger and Clell Miller.

Kerry later said Cole had mentioned that the James brothers had come up with the plan. Jesse had convinced Bob that Minnesota would make a good target, and Bob convinced his older brother Cole. Bob had settled on a farm in Missouri with a woman and wanted to make some money before going straight. Cole was reluctant at first, but when he realized Bob would

WILLIAM STILES (MANY ALIASES, INCLUDING BILL CHADWELL) (UNKNOWN–SEPTEMBER 7, 1876)

An obscure outlaw, Stiles grew up in Monticello, Minnesota, and played a key role in convincing the gang to attempt a robbery there. Stiles had a long record of crime, including petty theft, passing counterfeit currency, and stealing horses. He spent some time in jail for this last offense. Stiles was a latecomer to the gang, only being involved in the Otterville and Northfield hold-ups.

The November 4, 1876 edition of the *Blue Earth City Post* reported, "Chadwell [aka Stiles], one of the men killed while attempting to rob the Northfield bank, is undoubtedly the same man who worked in the tin and lead mines near this place two years ago. He was regarded as a desperate character. To illustrate his recklessness and daring it is related that on one occasion he, in company with another miner, got on a spree, and while standing around a fire Chadwell's partner picked up a full keg of blasting powder and deliberately threw it on the fire. Chadwell very coolly slapped him over, and then snatched the keg of powder from the flames and threw it in the ditch. This circumstance is well known to many of our citizens."

Stiles was killed outside the bank at Northfield by A.R. Manning. His body was taken for dissection by Henry Wheeler.

go regardless, he decided to go along. Another story has it that it was all Bill Stiles' idea. This seems more likely since he was the only one familiar with Minnesota. He apparently filled the gang members' heads with visions of peaceful, compliant citizens, and rich, unguarded banks.

Frank, Jesse, and Cole were all experienced robbers and former bushwhackers. Clell Miller's wartime record wasn't impressive but he had ridden along on some of the gang's jobs. He'd also shown a talent for getting out of tight spots. On March 26, 1875, Clell was in Carrolton, Missouri, recovering from a leg wound. Three Pinkerton agents and Sheriff John Clinkscales tried to arrest him. He hid in a house and the Pinkertons threatened to burn it down. Clinkscales entered the house to reason with Miller but the outlaw captured him and, using the poor sheriff as a crutch, hobbled to a getaway horse and safety.

Bob Younger was less experienced, as was Bill Stiles. Bob was a trusted brother, though, and Stiles was important for his knowledge of the many small roads and villages of southern Minnesota. By September the wheat harvest would have already been sold at market, so the farmers would have deposited plenty of money in the banks. The bushwhackers must have worried about being so far from home with only one local guide and no friends, but the temptation proved to be too much.

Canada was also suggested as an option, the assumption being that Canadians wouldn't fight like Americans, but since none of the gang members were familiar with the country they decided to go with Minnesota. While far from Missouri, its very distance from the previous robberies would make the people easier to surprise. Or so their reasoning went.

The gang didn't take any chances, though, and went heavily armed. Jesse James liked to use the Smith & Wesson Schofield .45. He preferred single-action revolvers such as this model because with the hammer cocked,

Jesse James in a photograph taken in 1874 or 1875. He grew out his beard before the Northfield raid. (LoC)

it only took a light pull on the trigger to fire. Double-action revolvers needed a harder squeeze on the trigger that could affect a gunman's aim. Jesse carried several weapons. One gun retrieved at the scene of the robbery and said to have been carried by Jesse was a Colt M1862 round-barrel Conversion Pocket Navy. This was a .38 rimfire weapon.

Several members of the gang liked the M1851 Colt Navy revolver, an old favorite among bushwhackers. This .36-caliber weapon only weighed 42oz, so many bushwhackers carried several. They also carried the Colt M1873 Army revolver. Dubbed the "Peacemaker," this .45 revolver was single-action and weighed 1.05kg (37oz). Cole Younger carried at least one, as it was recovered from him after he was captured.

Bloody Bill Anderson gave Frank and Jesse James a long lesson in brutality and fighting during the Civil War. Here he is shown in death, killed in action by a Union force. He wears a typical "guerrilla shirt" favored by Missouri bushwhackers. (LoC)

INITIAL STRATEGY

Funding the operation

The plan was a simple one, but required some serious preparation. They'd be going into territory unfamiliar to all but one of them and it was a long ride from Missouri. They needed provisions, horses, and spending money. Earning it was out of the question, so the gang decided to raise funds by robbing a train.

On July 7, 1876, the gang rode in groups of two westwards from California, Missouri, and met at around 2pm about two miles east of the Missouri Pacific Railroad Bridge across the Lamine River. The gang at this point included Frank and Jesse James, Bob and Cole Younger, Hobbs Kerry, Clell Miller, Charlie Pitts, and Bill Stiles.

Shortly after sunset, at about 9.30pm, they approached the bridge and captured the watchman. They then proceeded half a mile westward along the track to Rocky Cut, a manmade canyon cut through a hill two miles east of the town of Otterville. They were waiting for the Missouri Pacific No. 4 Express, going from Kansas City to St. Louis. It had the engine, two sleepers, three coaches, a baggage car, and an express car of the Missouri, Kansas and Texas Railroad containing two safes – one of the Adams Express Company and the other of the United States Express Company.

The train reached Rocky Cut at around 10.30pm. The bandits had piled railroad ties on the tracks in case the train didn't stop. As the train approached, the watchman was forced at gunpoint to flag it down with a red lantern while some members of the gang stood nearby and others stayed on the sides of the cut. The engineer didn't brake in time and the "engine climbed up on the ties, rising fully ten inches off the track, and then stopped and of its own weight settled back on the track." Kerry and Stiles hurried up behind the train and placed a barrier there too.

To intimidate the passengers and crew, the bandits whooped and fired shots in the air. They kept up such a fusillade that most witnesses estimated

JULY 7, 1876

The gang robs the Missouri Pacific No. 4 Express near Otterville, MO the gang at twice or three times their actual number. Anyone foolish enough to stick their head out the window to see what was going on was told in no uncertain terms to put it right back in again.

Two bandits boarded the engine and captured the engineer and fireman. Three others entered the express car side door, which was open in the hot summer evening. All but one of the robbers wore masks. The baggage master, a man named Conkling, was in the car and got captured. The express agent, J.B. Bushnell, had already fled to one of the sleepers where he convinced a brakeman to hide the keys in his shoe. Bushnell then sat down and pretended to be a passenger. Conkling was led through the train at gunpoint until he came to the agent and pointed him out. The guns swiveled from Conkling to Bushnell and the agent quickly pointed to the brakeman. The guns swiveled again.

The bandits marched all three back to the express car. They opened the United States Express Company safe and dumped the letters and packages into a wheat sack. None of the keys fit the Adams Express safe, however, because it was a "through" safe, meaning none of the packages were being delivered to any waystations. All were going to St. Louis and that's where the key was. One of the bandits retrieved the fireman's coal hammer (a short-handled combination pick and hammer) and knocked a hole through the side of the safe. A bandit tried to reach through the jagged hole and only managed to scrape himself. One of his comrades with smaller hands plucked out the contents and put them in the sack.

No images of the Missouri Pacific No. 4 Express are known to exist. This is the No. 76, built in 1875 at the cost of $6,600. It is a Type 8800 class, the same type as the No. 4. (Missouri State Archives)

The passengers, meanwhile, were in a state of panic. Some hid under their seats, others joined a prayer service led by a preacher, while the more practical hid their valuables. A woman began to cry and a male passenger reassured her that he'd protect her with his life, to which another passenger suggested, "Why, then, don't you go fight those fellows in front?" The lady's self-proclaimed knight in shining armor had no response to that. One of the robbers was overheard suggesting that they rob the passengers too, but another robber who appeared to be the leader said they'd already been there an hour and needed to go.

They did rob the newsboy's concession chest and its stock of snacks and cigars. An eyewitness account said, "The way the candy disappeared would have done credit to any seven-year old." The cigars disappeared at a similar rate. One hungry robber greedily munched one of the newsboy's pies, smearing the filling all over his face. Incensed at this robbery, the newsboy set off his pistol, possibly a Derringer. Nobody was hurt and the robbers laughed. "Hear that little son of a bitch bark!"

The detectives who foiled the Granby heist heard that Kerry had returned to that town after an absence and was now flashing a bundle of cash. They put two and two together and arrested him on July 31. By that time he only had $20 left, having lost the rest of it gambling. In exchange for a mild sentence (four years) he named all his accomplices and told the whole story of the Rocky Cut train robbery, also known as the Otterville robbery.

The gang then said "good-bye boys" to the crew, warned them of the blockage behind the train, and untied the watchman, who had been left bound and gagged beside the track during the entire affair. No passengers were robbed and nobody hurt, not even the newsboy who shot at them. This chivalrous behavior was in stark contrast to some of their other robberies and the bloodbath that was to come at Northfield. The gang rode off with about $15,000 in cash, bank drafts, and papers. The local United States Express agent claimed that much of the paper would be unredeemable and thus the bandits really only got about $8,000 or $9,000. Kerry later claimed his share was about $1,200, which supports the agent's assertion. On the other hand, given that Kerry was only a friend of a friend and claimed to have only stood lookout during the actual robbery, his share may have been smaller. The gang broke up into groups of three and crossed the Osage River near Warsaw to elude pursuit.

Robbery of the Missouri Pacific Express (overleaf)
On the night of July 7, 1876, eight members of the James–Younger gang robbed the Missouri Pacific No. 4 Express at Rocky Cut two miles east of Otterville, Missouri. This heist was to raise money for the Northfield raid. The gang blocked the tracks with a pile of cross-ties and forced the watchman from a nearby railroad bridge to flag down the train with a red lantern, the signal for an emergency stop. The watchman was left tied up by the side of the track while two bandits captured the engineer and fireman. Three more entered the express car and forced the employees to open one of the two safes. Nobody had a key to the other safe so it had to be broken open with the fireman's coal hammer.

While all this was going on, two bandits piled more cross-ties behind the train so it couldn't get away, and a constant firing into the air was kept up to intimidate the passengers. Many passengers hid their valuables or joined in a prayer service led by a traveling preacher. No passengers were robbed but the newsboy's concession chest was plundered. The teenager was so outraged by this that he tried to shoot one of the robbers with his Derringer, to no effect.

THE PLAN

Jim Younger, who had refused to be a part of the Rocky Cut affair, was convinced to come along to Minnesota to replace Hobbs Kerry. He had been living within the law for some time and was reluctant to restart his life in crime. He worried about his younger brother Bob, though, and decided to go along to keep him safe. Jim was a seasoned ex-bushwhacker and made a good replacement for the less-experienced and obviously weaker Kerry.

The Otterville train robbery provided the money for the raid. All eight members of the gang rode blooded horses and were well equipped with at least two revolvers each and plenty of ammunition. Judging from accounts of the weeks leading up to the Northfield robbery, they carried along plenty of spending money as well.

The route of their approach to Northfield is uncertain. Reports of their movements are various, incomplete, and contradictory. Some accounts have the men all riding from Missouri to Minnesota in one or more groups. Another account has them sharing a wagon. Cole Younger, while always happy to speak to reporters in the years after the heist, gave differing accounts of their journey and of the robbery itself.

Another account says only Frank, Jesse, and Bill Stiles rode. Frank had recently purchased a dun-colored mare and thought it so fine that he wanted it for the robbery. The rest of the gang took the train to Minnesota, either with their horses in the stock car or without their mounts and bought horses there. Some accounts tell of men matching their description buying horses in Minnesota.

This last method of approach is the most likely. Frank and Jesse wanted to ride with Stiles in order to get to know him better and see the lay of the land. This also allowed Frank to use his cherished horse. Since the James brothers had become famous train robbers, perhaps they wanted to avoid riding one on the way to a job. If they were recognized at a station, news of their whereabouts could be telegraphed to the next station and lawmen could be waiting for them. The James brothers would be trapped in the train.

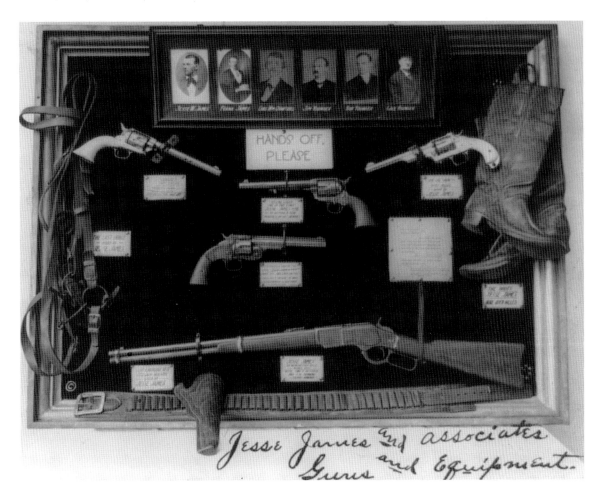

Jesse James and associates Guns and Equipment.

Having the others ride to Minnesota by twos or threes would reduce people's suspicions of the sudden appearance of a large number of well-armed strangers. It would also give part of the gang familiarity with the entire route – in fact more than one – from Missouri to Minnesota. Alternatively, coming by train would mean they'd have fresh mounts in Minnesota.

The gang had done similar approaches to targets before, once as far away as West Virginia. They would often pretend they were looking for land to buy. This gave them the excuse to ask lots of questions about local roads, towns, and natural barriers such as rivers and swamps. All accounts of the set up to this robbery and others say that the outlaws were generally friendly and well-behaved, acting sociably with the locals in order to put them at ease and get them to talk. They also invested in good maps of the area.

At least some of the gang, probably Cole Younger and Bill Stiles, arrived in Minneapolis in mid-August and spent a week seeing the town and living it up. There was a tense moment when Stiles was recognized by police officer Patrick Kenny, who had arrested him several years before in Iowa for one of his many crimes. Stiles gave Kenny a story about having gone straight. Whether Kenny believed this or not is unknown, but, since Stiles wasn't currently wanted in the state, the officer let him go.

"Relics of the James gang" on display in the 1920s. Items once "owned" by the bandits are displayed all over the U.S., most of them of doubtful provenance. This author has seen dozens of guns Jesse James supposedly used. The now-defunct Million Dollar Museum in New Mexico used the clever term, "said to have been owned by Jesse James." It's unlikely anyone but the museum owner ever said that! (LoC)

HOBBS KERRY (CAREY?) (1853?–UNKNOWN)

Perhaps less is known about Hobbs Kerry than any other member of the James–Younger gang. He rode with the gang for only one job – the Otterville train robbery – and was arrested for that. That earns him the dubious distinction of being the briefest and least successful member of the gang.

While Kerry was only 23 at the time of the Otterville robbery, he had already been in trouble with the law on more than one occasion. Kerry grew up in the lead mining town of Granby, Missouri, where he and his two brothers got into no end of trouble. His brother Toby was killed over a card game at a prostitutes' camp in 1870 and his other brother Albert killed a man over an argument about another prostitute the following year. Somehow Albert became city marshal in 1873. It wasn't long before he, Hobbs, and another man were arrested

over yet another murder. They were eventually released due to a lack of evidence.

Hobbs had his first brush with the James–Younger gang in 1875 when he met Bruce Younger, half-uncle to the Younger brothers. He also met Charlie Pitts and Bill Stiles. This led to the Granby bank robbery plan and eventually the Otterville job. Kerry was arrested and gave a full confession. Jesse James, or someone writing under his name, penned a letter to the papers calling Kerry a "notorious liar and poltroon" and claiming Jesse had many witnesses who would swear he wasn't there that day.

After his four years in prison for the Otterville affair, this obscure member of the gang faded into even greater obscurity. Even his date of death is unknown.

JULY 31, 1876

Hobbs Kerry arrested

EARLY TO MID-AUGUST

The gang heads to Minnesota. Their exact route is uncertain

Younger and Stiles went to the Chinn and Morgan gambling house in nearby St. Paul to try their luck. The experienced bandits were in over their heads, though, and got fleeced of $200 or $300 by some local card players. It was a hot day, and the booze and the crowd inside the gambling house made it hotter. To cool themselves and send a message, Younger and Stiles took off their coats to reveal an arsenal of pistols and knives. The local gamblers made sputtered protests that they weren't cheating and the proprietor asked the two to cover up their weapons.

Then the proprietor did a double-take. He recognized Stiles as the same man who had palmed off some counterfeit bills in his place several years earlier. He decided not to confront the rough characters, however, since they weren't getting rowdy and he wanted to keep it that way. The September 10, 1876 edition of the *St. Paul Dispatch* reported, "While on the visit in question, they were asked, in thieves' parlance, if they were 'working the trains,' that is, were they engaged in burglarious or similar attempts? To this they gave a tacit acknowledgement."

Since this report was written after the robbery, this might have been a case of 20/20 hindsight. It's hard to believe that seasoned outlaws would make such a slip, but considering that Stiles was playing cards in an establishment where he'd been seen passing counterfeit notes, perhaps it's not so unbelievable after all. One of the persistent illusions of the outlaw legend is that the famous bad men of the Wild West were any more capable than anyone else. Often they were simply more daring. That was the case with Doc Holliday, considered by many to be one of the best shootists of the West while in reality he was only mediocre. He was terminally ill, however, and that gave him a level of courage other men lacked. Another odd report about Younger and

Stiles was that two men who fit their descriptions were discovered sleeping in a ditch the next morning.

Some reports have Bob Younger and Clell Miller arriving by train on August 19 and buying horses the next day. They visited several livery stables and asked around to get the best deal, even, according to one story, asking the local marshal and deputy for advice. All four outlaws spent a few more days in town, eating at fine restaurants and gambling.

Soon the rest of the gang arrived. The owner of the hotel where they stayed noted they all wore white linen dusters and white hats and looked tough, although they claimed they were members of the Grange, an agricultural association. At other times they claimed they were looking to buy cattle or searching for a new railroad route. They looked too tough and rich to be Grangers or engineers, however, and the money they spent and weapons they carried told a different story. They also had the odd habit of standing on the hotel balcony and dropping 50-cent or dollar coins down into the crowd below.

The Southern view of Benjamin Butler. This drawing shows depicts Maj. Gen. Butler, military governor of New Orleans from May to December 1862, shown as Bluebeard for challenging the behavior of the city's Confederate women toward Union soldiers. "John Bull" looks on in horror. If Southerners hoped Butler's actions would prompt England to come into the war on the side of the South, they were disappointed. England did protest the General Order No. 28 but took no action. (LoC)

As odd and suspicious as this behavior was, the strangers were always polite and paid their bills, so nobody could quite find fault with them. One wonders if tales of their antics were exaggerated for the papers in the excitement of the robbery's aftermath. It is impossible to say.

It was now late August and the band decided their vacation was over and it was time to get to work. Knowledge of their movements is sketchy. In the days after the robbery, the newspapers were full of interviews with farmers, hoteliers, and shopkeepers who had met some or all of the outlaws. It's uncertain how many of these reports are true and picking out those that are would be an impossible task. Northfield expert John Koblas has dubbed these nebulous accounts "Jesse sightings."

Several reports tell of their generosity, giving lavish tips and buying people drinks. Others tell of their buying horses and maps, and remarked on their fine steeds and horsemanship. As at St. Paul, they claimed to be cattlemen, railroad surveyors, or land speculators, basically any trade that gave them an excuse to ask a lot of questions about roads and terrain. None reported seeing the gang all together, so it seems they traveled in small groups. This was a common bushwhacker tactic – to split up and rendezvous later for an attack, and then split up again.

While the gang's movements in Minnesota are open to question, they appear to have cased several towns across the state. They decided against western Minnesota because the region had recently been blighted by locusts. They reasoned that with the farmers depositing no money, and indeed having to take more out to meet expenses, the pickings would be lean in that part of the state.

Red Wing, a town in southeast Minnesota and only about 35 miles east of Northfield, had three rich banks but proved unsuitable because there

Benjamin Butler as a Congressman from Massachusetts. He served from 1867 to 1875 and again from 1877 to 1879. (LoC)

were only two roads out of town. The veteran bushwhackers always wanted a variety of options for getting out of trouble. Mankato was another possibility but a Board of Trade meeting was going on near the bank so there were too many potential witnesses. In Mankato, a teller at the First National Bank was confronted with a large man who asked to have a $20 bill changed, a normal request at that time but a common tactic of the James gang to case a bank. The teller gave him four $5 bills and noticed that the man counted his bills slowly and gave the vault and the rest of the building a good looking over. A guard was posted at the bank that evening.

Two witnesses claim to have recognized Jesse James in Minnesota before the robbery. One was a madam in St. Paul who went by the name Mollie Ellsworth and whose real name was Kitty Traverse. The September 20, 1876 edition of the *St. Paul Pioneer Press* reported that Jesse visited her brothel along with two other men. Jesse recognized her as being the same woman who had run a house of ill-repute in St. Louis. She noted that he carried three or four large pistols. Kitty asked Jesse if he was planning any jobs in Minnesota and the bandit replied that he wasn't. Kitty didn't believe him and to cover herself from any culpability, mentioned the visit to local law enforcement. She didn't mention exactly who had visited her. Snitching on the James gang was tantamount to suicide. The police appear to have done nothing.

The second witness who recognized Jesse was Charles Robinson of Mankato, who saw him riding down Main Street of that town. Robinson knew Jesse from his time living in Missouri and noted that the outlaw wore a thick black moustache and beard. He called out to Jesse, but the outlaw ignored him and kept riding. This was reported in the *Mankato Weekly Review* on September 12.

Eventually the gang settled upon Northfield, a prosperous town south of St. Paul that boasted a sawmill, many shops, a girls' college, and rich farmland untouched by locusts, so the banks should be stuffed with money.

A contemporary account by journalist Joseph Have Hanson, who under the pseudonym John Jay Lemon wrote an account of the robbery just weeks after the events titled *The Northfield Tragedy*, describes the town:

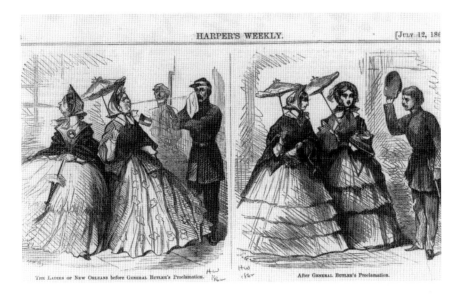

HARPER'S WEEKLY. [JULY 12, 186

THE LADIES OF NEW ORLEANS before GENERAL BUTLER'S Proclamation. After GENERAL BUTLER'S Proclamation.

A very different view of Butler's order was taken by the Northern press. This image from the July 12, 1862 edition of *Harper's Weekly* shows how New Orleans women treated Union officers before the proclamation and after. While this is obviously propaganda, the order does appear to have reduced harassment of the occupying troops. In fact, after Butler captured New Orleans in May of 1862, the city remained remarkably orderly throughout the war. (LoC)

Northfield is a thriving, pretty little village, situated pleasantly upon both banks of the Cannon river just 35 miles from St. Paul in Rice County, on the St. Paul and Milwaukee railroad. A neat iron bridge unites the northwest and southeast sides of the town, and just above the bridge is one of the finest mill races in the State, the water in its incessant flow roaring like the ocean and appearing like a miniature Niagara. There is a large flouring mill on either side of the river belonging to Messrs. Ames & Co. The public school buildings are not surpassed in the State for their beauty of design and adaptability of construction, and the Carlton college is another institution of which the town may well be proud. Placed as it is in the center of a rich farming district, the citizens are considered well-to-do, and the bank transacts a large business.

There was also another motive for picking Northfield. It was the home of Adelbert Ames, formerly Brigadier-General Ames of the Union army, who served under the notorious Major-General Benjamin "Beast" Butler. Given command of New Orleans in 1862, Butler became the symbol of Yankee oppression to Southerners thanks to the wholesale corruption of his administration. Homes were looted, illegal trade in cotton with supposedly secessionist planters became big business, and any woman who bothered Union soldiers was told she would be labeled and treated as a "lady of the evening." This last bit inspired a Southern entrepreneur to manufacture chamber pots with Butler's face on them.

By the rebels' way of thinking, anyone associated with Butler was a damned Yankee. Ames became a twice-damned Yankee when he served as a "carpetbag" senator to Mississippi starting in 1869. In 1870 he married Butler's daughter Blanche. In Mississippi he tried to suppress the Klan and give blacks equal rights. In 1874 he was elected governor with a black man, A.K. Davis, as lieutenant governor. Ames proved no match for the backstabbing world of Reconstruction politics, however, and soon faced impeachment over what appear to be false charges of corruption and misuse of power. Disgusted with the Deep South, he resigned and went as far away from it as he could and still remain in the country – to Northfield, Minnesota. There he bought a share in his father's flour mill and set to work on a new life.

Northfield may have been the outlaws' target all along. As Cole Younger wrote in his memoirs, "General Benjamin F. Butler, whom we preferred to call 'Silver Spoons' Butler from his New Orleans experiences during the war, had a lot of money invested, we were told, in the First National Bank at Northfield, as had J.T. Ames [*sic*], Butler's son-in-law … we felt little compunction under the circumstances, about raiding him or his."

One story has it that Cole Younger fled to Jacksonville, Florida, for a time and overheard some people talking about how Butler had deposited $300,000 in stolen Southern money in a bank in Northfield. This is almost certainly a later invention since by their movements it seems clear that the gang hadn't settled on raiding Northfield when they came to Minnesota. It appears Cole Younger and Bill Stiles cased Northfield just before the robbery and were satisfied that the bank appeared prosperous. It might have been encouraging that they found no gun shop in town. They went to tell their comrades they had found their target.

AUGUST 19

Some reports say Bob Younger and Clell Miller arrived by train at St. Paul on this day and buy horses on August 20

LATE AUGUST

The gang scouts out possible targets in Minnesota. Their movements are unclear

THE RAID

On Thursday morning, September 7, the gang came together again at Dundas, three miles southwest of Northfield. They rode unhurriedly to Northfield, three of them arriving at around 11 in the morning. Most scholars say the three were Bob Younger, Pitts, and either Frank or Jesse. Two more bandits soon followed. After a brief look around, they went back over the river to D.E. Jefts' Railroad Restaurant next to the railway station and ate a lunch of ham and eggs. The rest of the gang was reported to have eaten at John Tosney's Eating Establishment. Ordering lunch in a town they were planning to rob that same day was a brazen act; some might say a foolish one.

According to some accounts, two of the bandits, identified as Frank James and Bob Younger, went to the Exchange Saloon on Division Street, just up the street from the bank, and got drunk. After downing a fair amount of booze, they remembered they had a job to do, ordered a quart of whiskey to go, and rejoined their friends.

After lunch, three bandits rode back into town. They all wore white linen dusters. At around 2pm they crossed a bridge over the Cannon River that leads to Mill Square. On the bridge they passed Adelbert Ames riding with his brother John. The Ames brothers had just been to the bank and were returning to the family mill. Adelbert heard one of the strangers say to another, "There is Governor Ames himself."

Adelbert Ames turned to his brother and said, "Those men are from the South and here for no good purpose. No one here calls me Governor."

The three hitched their horses and sat down on some dry goods boxes in front of Lee and Hitchcock's store, located next door to the bank on the corner of Division Street and Mill Square. This gave a good view of the bank, the street, the square, and the bridge. The three are identified as Charlie Pitts, Bob Younger, and Frank James. Soon Clell Miller and Cole Younger rode into view from across the bridge. Miller, relaxed about the whole affair, was coolly smoking a pipe. Their arrival was

SEPTEMBER 7, 2PM

The gang attempts to rob the bank at Northfield

Maj. Gen. Adelbert Ames, taken while he served in the Federal Army during the Civil War. As an artillery lieutenant during the Battle of Bull Run, he was seriously wounded but refused to leave his guns. This heroism earned him the Medal of Honor, although it wasn't awarded until 1893. By war's end he had been brevetted a major general in the Union army and a brigadier general in the regular army. He served again in the Spanish–American War. Ames died in 1933 at age 97, the last surviving general officer of the Civil War. (LoC)

the signal for the three to enter the bank. Cole Younger recalled:

When Miller and myself crossed over the bridge, I saw a crowd of citizens about the corners, also our boys sitting there on some boxes. I remarked to Miller about the crowd and said, "Surely the boys will not go into the bank with so many people about. I wonder why they did not ride straight through the town." We were half way across the square when we saw the three men rise and walk up the sidewalk towards the bank. Miller said: "They are going in," and I replied, "If they do the alarm will be given as sure as there's a hell, so you had better take that pipe out of your mouth."

Just then the rest of the gang – Jim Younger, Jesse James, and Bill Stiles – crossed the bridge. The robbery was going to happen whether Cole wanted it to or not.

It was Cole Younger and Clell Miller's job to guard the entrance to the bank. Trying to look casual, Miller got off his horse in front of the bank, approached the door, glanced inside, closed the door, and stood guard. Cole stayed in the middle of the street standing next to his horse, pretending to adjust its saddle girth. While some passersby were looking curiously at the newcomers, noting their fine horses and matching white linen dusters, most didn't think anything serious was going on. A few sharp-eyed folks watched the newcomers keenly. There was something a bit too martial about their bearing, a bit too deliberate about their actions. Nobody did anything until J.S. Allen, owner of one of the hardware stores in town, approached the bank. He had noticed the men crossing the bridge and had grown suspicious. He decided to peek into the bank to see if everything was all right. Clell Miller grabbed him, put a gun to his face, and told him not to move, saying, "You son of a bitch, don't you holler."

But holler he did. Either bravely or stupidly depending on your opinion, Allen tore out of Miller's grasp and ran around the corner yelling, "Get your guns boys! They're robbing the bank!" Several others took up the call. Miller shot several bullets over Allen's head and the whole plan started to fall apart.

H.B. Gress, another local, said that, "Up to that time I had no idea what was to occur. I hollered at once, 'They are robbing the bank.' And it was taken up from store to store until the whole business part of the town was aroused to the situation."

A medical student named Henry Wheeler started shouting too. He was visiting his family in Northfield while on vacation from the University of Michigan. As Clell Miller leapt on to his horse, Younger ordered Wheeler to move away and fired a couple of shots over his head to emphasize the point.

The iron suspension bridge over the Cannon River. This is the view the gang had as they rode over this bridge and on to Mill Square beyond. (Northfield Historical Society)

If the citizens of Northfield hadn't been paying attention, they certainly were now. Younger and Miller galloped up and down the street ordering everyone to get inside and firing into the air. Cole had used similar intimidation tactics numerous times during their bushwhacker years when raiding towns and hamlets. Back then it generally worked. This time it didn't.

Albert T. Dutcher had the bad timing to be visiting Northfield on business from Pittsburgh. He told the September 13 edition of the *St. Peter Tribune*:

At 2:10pm, on Thursday the seventh, as I was standing at the foot of the stairs of the Dampier House in Northfield, Minnesota, looking across Mill Square in the direction of the iron bridge, I noticed four men on horseback crossing the bridge and coming up across Mill Square towards me. As there was nobody else on the street coming from that direction, I noticed them more particularly than I otherwise would have done.

As they approached at the foot of Main Street, which crosses Mill Square, not to exceed four rods from where I stood, I noticed them very suddenly wheel about their horses, with revolvers in their hands, three shooting into the air and one of the ruffians, noticing me standing alone at the corner of the hotel, aimed at me with his revolver and cried out, "You son of a bitch, get back there," and fired at the same time, the ball striking in the corner of the hotel, very near to where I was standing. His warning seemed to allow me just time to dodge behind a corner of the hotel before he shot. I obeyed his order very quickly, as the four shots seemed to be discharged in rapid succession. I dodged my head out from the corner and saw two men standing in the door of the bank with drawn revolvers.

Dutcher appears to be mistaken about the number of people he saw crossing the bridge. Most accounts, including Cole Younger's, have three of the gang crossing, then two more, then the final three. Considering Dutcher's brush with death and the ensuing chaos, this mistake is forgivable.

Henry Wheeler, hero and grave robber of Northfield. (Northfield Historical Society)

A hue and cry went up among the citizens of Northfield. Those who had guns grabbed them. Wheeler was one of the first to act. An avid hunter, he owned a gun but it was at his home several blocks away. The medical student suddenly remembered an old army rifle and sack of cartridges behind the desk of the Dampier House, a hotel across the street and a little to the north of the bank. Wheeler started running towards it and Miller took a shot at him. Cole Younger shouted, "Don't shoot him; let him go." In later years Cole always insisted he never wanted to shoot any bystanders unless forced to. Considering his previous record, this may have been the case, but the situation was getting beyond his control.

Continuing unscathed, Wheeler rushed into the hotel and found the owner standing behind the counter. He grabbed the gun – a breech-loading, single-shot .50-caliber Smith carbine left over from the Civil War – but Dampier only found three cartridges. Wheeler hurried up to a third-floor window.

Once he got there he saw that five robbers were now riding up and down Division Street, shooting at anyone who showed themselves and telling everyone to get in. Bullets smashed through windows or punched holes into walls and columns. Into the midst of this chaos strolled Nicolaus Gustavson, a Swedish immigrant and blacksmith. Some reports say he didn't understand English; others that he was drunk. Perhaps both reports were true. He stood in plain view staring at the bandits. Oddly enough, a Wild West show was planned for that evening, so he might have thought this was part of it. Enraged that Gustavson wasn't listening, one of the robbers shot him in the head. Gustavson staggered away mortally injured and died four days later. At least one witness said that the bandit who fired the fatal shot was the one giving orders outside the bank and calling to his comrades inside, which would mean it was Cole Younger.

One onlooker, R.C. Phillips, observed two wildly different reactions from the citizens of Northfield. "While the shooting was going on in the street and most people were seeking the shelter of a friendly wall, Elias Hobbs (former chief of police), Col. Streeter, and a colored man named Ben Richardson stood on the Central Hotel corner, across the street, and threw rocks at the robbers. The chief of police, they say, was hid in a dry goods box back of Skinner & Drew's and did not come out until after the battle was over."

More effective were those who had guns handy. Elias Stacy got the first hit when he blasted a load of birdshot into Clell Miller's face. The impact pitched Miller from his horse but didn't actually do any grave harm. He was soon up and fighting again. Other snipers fired too, and soon the bandits were ducking and weaving, firing back to little effect. Since it was hunting season for prairie chickens, several Northfield residents had shotguns ready,

CLELLAND B. "CLELL" MILLER (UNKNOWN–SEPTEMBER 7, 1876)

Clell Miller is one of the more mysterious members of the James–Younger gang. Even his name and date of birth are uncertain. Various sources refer to him as Cleland Miller, Clenand Miller, and McClelland Miller and give his date of birth as January 9, 1850, December 15, 1849, or September 1850 according to the census. His grave spells his name Clelland Miller and gives his birth date as December 15, 1849. His date of death is certain, as it was witnessed by the entire town of Northfield.

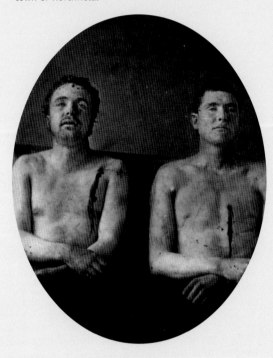

Bill Stiles and Clell Miller, propped up in a photographer's studio after being killed on Division Street outside the bank at Northfield. While it seems grim to us today, photographs of dead outlaws were taken and circulated as mementoes. This also served the practical purpose of helping in their identification. (Northfield Historical Society)

Miller was born in Kearney, Missouri, just a few miles from the James farm. He was wounded and captured by Union forces in 1864 during an ambush of Bloody Bill Anderson's gang, in which Anderson and several other bushwhackers were killed. Miller, then a teenager, claimed he had been forced to ride along with them and had been an unwilling part of the band for only four days. Miller stated, "I have always been a loyal boy and never sympathized with the South." His father and neighbors attested to his innocence and Miller was released from prison in April 1865. This poor start to his career didn't dissuade him, and he ended up riding with more experienced bushwhackers after the war as an outlaw. Miller was said to have been the joker of the gang, good-looking, good-natured, and always ready to laugh, even though he fought hard at Northfield.

He may have been part of the gang's 1871 robbery of a train at Corydon, Iowa, a crime for which he was caught, tried, and acquitted. He is reported to have been at other robberies too, but little is known for sure until his certain involvement in the Otterville and Northfield jobs. He was killed outside the bank at Northfield by Henry Wheeler. After Northfield, Jesse James recruited Clell's younger brother Edward (1856?–1881?) into the gang. He was there when Jesse robbed the Glendale train and on other jobs and was allegedly killed by Jesse in 1881 for talking too much, although another story has it that he went into hiding and lived a full life.

Clell Miller managed to have a full life even after death. Henry Wheeler was a medical student at the University of Michigan at Ann Arbor. He and two fellow medical students commandeered the bodies of Miller and Stiles to use for dissection. At that time it wasn't possible for doctors to get cadavers legally so doctors and students often bought them from grave robbers. Once Wheeler became a doctor, he kept Miller's skeleton in his office as a curio.

loaded with birdshot. While this wouldn't kill a tough bandit, it was painful, distracting, and quickly sapped the gang's morale.

Suddenly the tide had shifted. Everyone started getting in on the game. Despite what Stiles had assured his accomplices, the Minnesotans weren't afraid of the bandits. One resident later told the press he was out hunting and regretted he had missed out on the "fun."

Manning fired from the foot of the stairs going up the side of this building. Bob Younger hid behind some boxes underneath these stairs as he tried to shoot Manning. Instead he took a shot from Wheeler that shattered his right elbow. The triple-arched entrance to the bank can be seen behind the horse and cart in the center of the picture. The horse is tethered to one of the same three posts used by the three bandits who entered the bank to tether their own horses. (Northfield Historical Society)

Two butchers who had a shop on the south side of Mill Square saw the trouble, emptied the till, and retreated to the smokehouse. They were found an hour after the shooting stopped, still in their smokehouse, ready to defend their sides of beef with meat cleavers. A similar incident occurred at the all-female Carleton College. One of the matrons, hearing the shootout, ran into the college yelling, "Keep the girls off the street," and promptly fainted. The trustee's wife gathered the girls, armed each one with an axe, and took them all to the third floor to make a last stand for feminine virtue.

Henry Wheeler was now ready at the window, with a good view of Division Street and the bandits below. He recalled, "As I approached the window, three … men on horseback came riding up across the bridge square, shooting."

He fired a shot at them but missed. As he reloaded, he got some help in the form of A.R. Manning, who ran the hardware store next to the bank.

A Remington rolling-block rifle of the type Manning used against the Northfield robbers. This single-shot rifle was widely popular from its introduction in 1867 until the 1890s for both civilian and military use and was copied in several countries including Norway, the Papal States, and Egypt. Some accounts have Manning using a Winchester rolling-block rifle, which is of a very similar pattern. (Piero Crociani Collection)

"When I first heard the shooting," Manning said, "I thought these men had gotten permission to ride through the streets shooting blanks to call attention to a Wild West show [scheduled for later in the day]. Then I heard someone shout, 'robbing the bank.' I had been practicing with my rifle [a single-shot, breech-loading Winchester] the spring before and knew exactly what it would do, so I ran back and got it, stuffed a handful of cartridges in my pocket and ran back to the corner, loading on the way."

Taking up a position behind some stairs at the corner of Mill Square and Division Street, Manning started a calm and deadly fire at the bandits. Wheeler and Manning weren't the only ones firing. Adelbert Ames recalled that, "Every old musket, shot gun, and pistol was drawn from its hiding place."

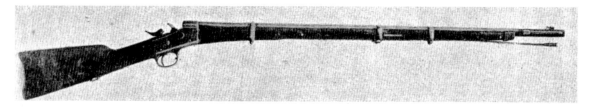

Having reloaded, Wheeler aimed out of his vantage point. Clell Miller, bleeding from the birdshot lodged in his face, had gotten back in the saddle. Miller spotted Wheeler and snapped a shot at the medical student, missing. Wheeler took careful aim and shot Miller through the chest, killing him.

Cole Younger recalled, "Miller called to me, saying he was shot, and looking at him I saw the blood running down his face [from the birdshot fired by Elias Stacy]. The firing by this time had become general, and as the two men in the bank had not yet come out, I was forced for the third time to ride to the bank and call to them to come out. And this time they did so. In the meantime, Miller had been shot again [by Wheeler] and had fallen from his horse. I jumped from my horse, ran to Miller to see how badly he was hurt, and, while turning him over, was shot in the left hip."

The shot that hit Cole was fired by Manning, who in short order also killed Pitts' horse – which the bandit had been using as a living shield – and shot Bill Stiles dead through the heart. Stiles toppled to the ground in front of Lockwood's store, almost an entire block away, showing that Manning had indeed practiced with his rifle.

All this accurate firing earned Manning some special attention. Eyewitnesses estimated that more than 30 shots were fired in his direction. A set of wooden stairs next to the corner where Manning stood was riddled with bullets. Little did Manning know that he was losing his backup. Wheeler, up in the hotel, had pulled out his third and last cartridge, a special paper-and-foil type, and found it torn and useless. He was out of ammunition.

But other Northfield citizens were getting into the battle. Several sources noted the brave but peculiar actions of Mr. G.E. Bates, who worked opposite the bank. All Bates had to hand was a jammed shotgun and an empty revolver, so he stood behind the door jamb calling out, "Now I've got you" while aiming at one or another of the robbers with the revolver. This distracted the bandits and they wasted much time and ammunition on him.

Others were firing with loaded guns. Nobody knows how many guns were aimed at the robbers that day, but none of the gang would leave town unscathed. With two men down and more taking hits every minute, the gang now realized it was time to run. Cole grabbed Miller's guns and remounted.

Inside the bank

Things inside the bank hadn't been going much better. Charlie Pitts, Bob Younger, and one of the James brothers, most likely Frank, made no show of being customers as they had in many of their earlier robberies. They simply drew their guns on the three employees and vaulted over the counter. The employees were teller Alonzo Bunker, bookkeeper and acting cashier Joseph Lee Heywood, and assistant bookkeeper Frank Wilcox.

One of the robbers said, "Throw up your hands. We are going to rob the bank. Don't any of you holler. We've got 40 men outside."

Wilcox observed later, "It was very evident that they had been drinking, as the smell of liquor was very strong."

The employees were ordered to their knees with their hands up. The robbers searched each man for weapons. Bob Younger felt a jackknife in

Robbing the First National Bank (overleaf)

As Bob Younger, Frank James, and Charlie Pitts entered the bank, Jesse James, Bill Stiles, Clell Miller, and Cole and Jim Younger stayed outside to control the crowd. The alarm was raised when a citizen tried to enter the bank and was warned away with a shot from Miller. People fetched their guns and started shooting at the bandits.

Here we see A.R. Manning firing from the corner of the Scriver building at the robbers. He has already killed one of the horses behind which a bandit was hiding. Henry Wheeler is firing from a third-story window of the Dampier House Hotel and killing Clell Miller, who had already taken a load of birdshot in the face, courtesy of another Northfield citizen. The rest of the gang is riding up and down the street firing at the townspeople. At first they had fired to scare them and get them off the streets, but once the civilians started shooting back the gang began firing in earnest. One passerby, Nicolaus Gustavson, has already taken a fatal head wound. Inside the bank, teller Alonzo Bunker is making his escape while Pitts is running after him. The other two employees, Wilcox and Heywood, are being questioned and roughed up by the rest of the gang but do not reveal the fact that the vault is unlocked.

Alonzo Bunker, teller at the First National Bank of Northfield. (Northfield Historical Society)

Assistant bookkeeper Frank Wilcox. (Northfield Historical Society)

Wilcox's pocket and asked what it was. When the bookkeeper replied it was only a jackknife, Bob Younger didn't bother to take it or even check if Wilcox was telling the truth. He and his companions rummaged around the counter for the cash drawer but only found a box with a small amount of money that they put in a grain sack. They missed the main cash drawer, situated just below the box, which held $2,000.

The robbers asked each man in turn if he was the cashier. All of them said no but then one robber turned to Heywood. He was the oldest and had been sitting behind a desk when they came in.

"You are the cashier," the bandit declared. "Open that safe quick or I'll blow your head off."

The vault had an outer and inner door. The outer one stood open and the inner was closed and unlocked, although there was no way of telling that by a casual glance. Pitts entered the vault and Heywood sprang to the door to shut him in. Another robber grabbed the cashier and yanked him away.

As this was happening, Bob Younger saw Bunker had moved closer to the counter. Younger spotted a small pistol there – a Smith & Wesson .32 caliber – and stepped between the teller and the weapon.

"You needn't try to get a hold of that. You couldn't do anything with that little derringer anyway," Younger mocked him as he put the pistol in his pocket.

Now thoroughly incensed, the three bandits ganged up on Heywood and ordered him to open the inner door.

"It has a time lock on it, and cannot be opened," Heywood bluffed.

The bandits told him he was a liar and started roughing him up.

"Murder! Murder! Murder!" Heywood shouted.

The bandits then commanded Wilcox and Bunker to unlock the vault, but they repeated the story that there was a time lock installed. One robber, said to be Frank James, knocked Heywood over the head with his gun and the cashier fell half-conscious on to the floor.

Pitts then drew a knife from his pocket and said, "Let's cut his damn throat."

Heywood, still stunned, made no movement as Pitts drew the knife along his throat. It was only meant to scare the cashier and left a slight scratch. Then they picked Heywood up and dragged him to the vault. They ordered him and the others to unlock it, which the employees said they couldn't do. As one historian has pointed out, they couldn't unlock a safe that wasn't locked in the first place! If the bandits had simply turned the latch and pulled, they would have been looking at $15,000.

In another attempt to scare Heywood, Pitts put his gun up to his head and fired, the bullet passing right by the cashier's head. Pitts let him go and he slumped back on the floor, still

An interior shot of the First National Bank of Northfield shortly after the robbery. (Northfield Historical Society)

stunned from being hit on the head. Bunker looked over at his coworker and felt sure Heywood had been shot and killed.

As they rummaged around and swore, the bandits' tempers grew shorter by the second. Bunker's nerve broke and he sprinted for the rear door, which was open but screened by some light shutters, a common feature for doors at that time to reduce dust coming in from the dirt roads outside. Bunker crashed right through the shutters with Pitts after him, firing at him once, the bullet hitting the blinds a moment before Bunker did. On the other side of the blinds stood a neighbor who had been peeking through to see what all the commotion was about. He got knocked head over heels.

The back exit led down some steps to an alley, down which Bunker ran. At the bottom of the steps he turned to sprint down the alley when Pitts fired again, the bullet lodging in Bunker's right shoulder. Bunker kept on running, and Pitts returned to the bank. Bleeding badly, the bookkeeper hurried through the back lot of the bank south to Fifth Street before making his way to the office of Doctor Coon on Water Street to get his wound seen to.

By this time, the robbers must have realized the heist had failed. Gunfire could be heard outside and they knew their comrades were having a hot time of it.

"Come out of the bank!" Cole Younger shouted from outside. "For God's sake, come out, they are shooting us all to pieces!"

Bob Younger came out first, leaving behind a bag of nickels he had collected. Manning saw him running up the sidewalk, straight for his position and aiming his revolver as he ran. Manning brought up his gun but

Acting cashier Joseph L. Heywood, hailed as the hero of Northfield Bank, killed September 7, 1876. (LoC)

Bob ducked behind some boxes under the stairs. Then Bob popped back out to shoot at Manning and the storeowner ducked behind the corner. Then it was Manning's turn to pop out and Bob's to duck back.

"We played hide and seek with the stairway between us," Manning said in an interview, "and I thought I had better get out of there. My idea was to go back through my store and get around behind him. Just then I saw his arm and leg kick out."

That was Wheeler's doing. The clerk at the hotel had performed some special room service in the form of extra ammunition and the medical student shot Bob through the right elbow, breaking it. Bob had enough presence of mind to do a "border shift," tossing his gun from his right hand to his left and continuing to fire at Manning. Then he spotted Bates waving his unloaded pistol from a doorway across the street. Thinking it was Bates who had shot him, Bob fired at him, grazing Bates in the face. Cole and Jim soon rode up and Jim helped Bob mount. Manning didn't know what was going on because he had started running around the block to get behind Bob. By the time he made it, the gang was already riding away.

Cole Younger recalled, "I then called to Pitts to help me get Miller up on my horse in front of me. On lifting him up we saw that he was dead, so I told Pitts to lay him down again and to run up the street out of range and I would take him up behind me."

The other two bandits in the bank also left, but before they did one of them fired at Heywood, who had risen to his feet and was staggering punch-drunk around the room. The shot hit Heywood in the head and killed him. The gang then fled, Pitts having to ride double behind Cole since his horse had been killed.

Escape from Northfield

The gang was in bad shape. Two of their members lay dead in the streets of Northfield, including the only one familiar with Minnesota. All of the gang members were wounded, Bob so seriously that he soon fainted and had to be held on his horse. Cole was shot in the hip, Jim in the shoulder, and Frank James in the leg. Pitts had also been hit. Jesse James was the last to be shot, getting a bullet in the thigh as the gang rode out of town. They were also short one horse.

That last problem was solved just outside Northfield. About halfway to Dundas, a town three miles southwest of Northfield, they stopped to wash

The north side of Mill Square, looking west across the iron suspension bridge taken as an escape route by the gang. Northfield's other bank stood in the set of buildings to the right. While it was slightly closer to the escape route, it had the disadvantage of not containing the money of two former Union generals. (Northfield Historical Society)

their wounds in a river and stole a horse from a passing farmer's team. The plodding plow horse wasn't anything like the blooded steed Pitts had lost back in town, but it would have to do. It also lacked a saddle, a shortcoming they fixed at the expense of another farmer shortly afterwards.

They could have gotten better horses just outside of town from Bill Revier, who had stopped his ice wagon at the home of a Mr. Foster. This Foster had hailed him to ask about all the shooting he heard in the distance. According to an interview Revier gave for the September 21, 1876 edition of the *Windom Reporter*, Revier and Foster, "…saw six of the gang riding toward us, two of them riding double – hence their need for another horse. They came toward us, their horses on a slow canter, and they were reloading their revolvers as they rode. As they neared me, I heard one of them say, 'Let's take a horse here,' while another said, 'No, no. Go on further.'"

It was good that they had hurried on, because they were already under pursuit. Two Northfield citizens had ridden after them almost immediately, using the horses Stiles and Miller would never need again. The pair came upon the gang just after they stole the plow horse. One of the robbers shouted at them to keep away, and the little posse, realizing they were outnumbered and way outgunned, obliged. They didn't run, though, and trailed the bandits from a safe distance.

Meanwhile back at Northfield, the citizens were in a flurry of activity. The bodies of the two bandits lay untouched on the street while men gathered weapons and horses and organized a posse. Items left behind by the bandits were quickly grabbed as curios. In the bank lay a white linen duster. Out in the street were a spur and two pistols. One pistol is still extant and is an 1872 Colt .45 with an ivory handle. A dead horse lay in front of the bank near Clell Miller's corpse. Bill Stiles lay further down the street. Several Northfield citizens made sympathetic noises about the horse while showing no pity for Miller and Stiles.

The telegraph lines hadn't been cut, a foolish oversight for veteran guerrillas, and soon news of the robbery flashed all across the region. A telegram reached St. Paul around 3pm, and the next train out an hour later carried a large number of police and reporters, who made it to the Northfield train station at 6.20pm.

The fugitives' first goal was Dundas, where a bridge offered them passage across the Cannon River. The town had been sent a telegraph message about the Northfield shootout but nobody was there to receive it. The telegraph operator was literally out to lunch. As the gang entered the village, onlookers overheard them cursing at each other, apparently blaming each one another for the disaster. A traveling salesman joked to the man next to him that they'd ride faster if Sitting Bull were after them. Not finding the joke funny, one of the gang whipped out a gun and shouted "Get in there, you son of a bitch!" Unlike the citizens of Northfield, the fellow ducked inside and did not grab a gun.

In this first stage of their flight the gang was not doing a good job of covering their tracks. They rode abreast, taking up the entire road and forcing farmers and their teams to give way, thus drawing attention to

themselves. In one case they ran an old man and his vegetable wagon off the road, leaving him stranded in a muddy ditch. Improvised bandages did little to stop a clearly visible trail of blood along the road. They stopped at one house for some water with which to wash their wounds and when the farmer asked what had happened to them, they said they had gotten into a gunfight with a gambler in Northfield and killed him. When the farmer asked the name of the man they shot, one cheekily replied that his name was Stiles.

The next town they passed through was Millersburg, six miles west of Dundas. Millersburg didn't have a telegraph station so the residents weren't aware of anything amiss. That's just as well for the bandits, because Millersburg was the home of Nicolaus Gustavson, who had fatally decided to visit Northfield on that day. The owner of the local inn recognized Bob and Cole Younger, Chadwell, and Pitts. They had stayed at his place the night before, claiming to be scouting the area for a new railroad. Shortly after the gang passed through town, the two Northfield residents pursuing

WAS THERE A NINTH ROBBER AT NORTHFIELD?

Every action by the James-Younger gang has gathered legends around it, and the Northfield raid is no exception. Since we've tried to assemble the most accurate narrative here, most such stories have been omitted, from the numerous "Jesse sightings" in the days leading up to the raid to a story of the gang's elaborately equipped secret cave hideaway in Minnesota. One tale, however, is worth telling, because it's the kind of story that enriches the folklore of the Wild West and maybe, just maybe, it's true.

The vast majority of historic and eyewitness accounts say there were eight robbers at Northfield, and Cole Younger's own account also supports this number. Yet a few eyewitnesses say there were nine men. At least one saw nine men ride over the bridge into Mill Square. Then there are the accounts that Frank and Jesse James, after they broke away from the rest of the gang to make their own way home, had a third rider with them.

Most people assumed the reports were in error and the idea of a ninth man was forgotten until 1913, when someone claiming to be Bill Stiles appeared in Los Angeles. Mainstream history relates that Bill Stiles, using the alias Bill Chadwell or Chadwick, died on the streets of Northfield on the day of the raid. One ripple in the theory that Stiles and Chadwell were the same person is a report that Stiles' father came all the way from his home in North Dakota to identify the body and went home relieved after seeing it wasn't his son.

The Bill Stiles who appeared in Los Angeles claimed that Chadwell and he had served as Confederate guerrillas together and were in fact two different people. Stiles claimed he had guarded the approach and getaway route at Northfield that day and wasn't involved in the shootout. Chadwell had indeed died at Northfield but Stiles got away. It should be noted that sightings of a ninth man only mention him crossing the bridge and riding with the James brothers during the getaway.

After Northfield, Stiles continued a life of crime, spent some time in prison, and was prowling around L.A. considering more robberies when he became nervous at the approach of a police officer on the street. He ducked into the Union Rescue Mission during services and hid among the parishioners. While listening to the sermon he became filled with the Holy Spirit and renounced his evil ways. He soon became the mission's night watchman, preventing crime rather than committing it.

In 1931, an aged Stiles spoke with pulp science-fiction and Western writer Ed Earl Repp and told his tale. Repp published the account, but Stiles complained the writer had added fiction to fact to make it more exciting. Whatever the truth of Stiles' tale, his fellow parishioners at the mission believed him, giving the simple reason that since Stiles was a Christian, he wouldn't lie.

So was there a ninth man at Northfield? We'll never know. It's a mystery.

And that's how legends should stay.

SEPTEMBER 7, AFTERNOON

The gang flees southwest, stealing horses to replace the ones they lost

them arrived in Millersburg and told everyone the news. They soon had 22 armed men join up with them. They continued on to Shieldsville, the route they correctly assumed the bandits were taking.

Meanwhile several towns were making hurried preparations for sending out posses. It did little good in the short term. The first posse to respond heard the news via telegraph at Faribault. Assuming the gang was headed to Shieldsville, about 15 miles southwest of Northfield, they hurried there and arrived before the robbers. They decided to wait in Haggerty's saloon, where they got busy drinking. Apparently Haggerty had a house rule of no weapons allowed, because the posse left all their firearms outside. The James-Younger gang soon showed up and went to wash their wounds at a water pump within sight of the saloon. Bob Younger fainted and fell off his horse. An old man sitting on Haggerty's porch gave them a strange look and the bandits explained Bob was a horse thief they had captured and were bringing to justice. The old man wasn't convinced and went inside to fetch the posse. The brave defenders of law and order hurried out, straight into the muzzles of the bandits. The gang told them not to interfere, shot up the pump, and left, leaving behind the posse's guns and horses.

This odd turn of events shows not only that the citizens of Faribault were far less capable of handling themselves than the townsmen of Northfield, but also that the bandits were not thinking clearly. Why shoot up the pump? Why not take the guns and horses? The gang were hurt, confused, and seemed to be in a panic. This sloppiness would soon catch up with them.

As the gang rode off, the posse went back into the saloon for more booze. Another, more disciplined, posse passed through town and pursued the gang. This posse numbered from ten to 15 men and caught up with the gang at a ravine about four miles west of Shieldsville. The bandits exchanged some shots with them before disappearing into the dense underbrush, a common escape route for bushwhackers during the war years. But before they could do that, Pitts fell off his horse when his saddle girth broke, which led to the false report that the posse had hit one of the outlaws. The horse, which was the plough horse they had earlier stolen, was allowed to go free. Not long afterwards Bob's saddle girth also snapped. He painfully mounted up behind Cole and rode double once again. Considering that he was barely conscious, it was probably best that he didn't ride his own horse.

By now the sun was setting. The pursuit would have to be continued the next day. All across the region, men polished up old shotguns and rifles, curried their horses, and gathered with their neighbors to make plans. Telegraph lines hummed with news of the outlaws' movements and plans for hunting them down.

To add to the outlaws' sufferings, a hard rain began to fall, which would continue with few breaks for the next two weeks. They continued on through a large old-growth forest called the Big Woods. This provided good cover, and the bandits took care to try to erase their tracks. It appears they slept in a farmer's barn or the woods that night. By dawn nearly a thousand men were after them in what many researchers say is the largest manhunt in American history. There was no real organization, no real plan, and so General Edmond Pope, who had fought with distinction on the Union side during the Civil War, was called in to help organize the pursuit. Living in Mankato, he was close to the scene and familiar with the territory.

Hunt for the gang

The manhunt was gaining momentum. The state offered $1,500 for each robber, and the bank offered an additional $500 per head. On September 12, Governor John S. Pillsbury threw in another $1,000. This encouraged more men to join the hunt. Prairie dogs were forgotten as the new game for the season was announced to be Missouri outlaws. Special police were brought down from St. Paul to join in the fun. At Faribault on September 9 a reporter observed:

SEPTEMBER 7, NIGHT

The gang sleeps either in a farmer's barn or in the woods

SEPTEMBER 8

Posses totaling about 1,000 men fan out across the area

The number of volunteers was larger than could be armed readily, and delay was caused by a search through the city for weapons. Everybody seemed willing and anxious to go to the front, and they came armed and mounted in every conceivable manner. A lad with a decrepit wooden leg came mounted on a bad-looking nag, and having a double-barreled fowling piece full of buckshot nearly to the muzzle, strapped on his back, while a horse-pistol stock peeped from his side pocket, he was accepted promptly, as his pluck was unquestionable.

Not all the posses were competent. The same article continues, "The Saint Paul boys are often mistaken for bandits, and the people run like mad … [they're] scared at the sight of a stump. One squad ran from Cannon River Ford. One man lost his false teeth. Another threw away his gun."

The September 9 edition of the *St. Paul & Minneapolis Pioneer-Press and Tribune* reported, "The last trace of them was found in a field near Waterville, where their tracks were discovered in a meadow. Here they doubled their tracks, and the scent was lost in the Big Woods. Many have an idea that they got away during the night and pressed on to the Minnesota River. Their horses were good for it, probably, except the one that carried double. The general impression is that they did not know the road; that the wounded man could not hold out, and that they are concealed in the Big Woods. Every bridge and road was guarded through the night, and if faithfully done, they could not have passed."

The gang's doubling their tracks and disappearing into the Big Woods shows that they had finally gotten their heads together and were actively trying to elude pursuit. One major barrier was the winding Cannon River, which was now flooded by the heavy rain. They tried several points along the river, asking locals for directions and passing themselves off as one of the many posses. At last they came to a bridge but found it guarded. Not wanting to get into a shootout, they continued on to Tetonka Lake, which they rode around.

At the opposite shore they came upon a large posse led by Captain Rogers. Both sides opened up a rapid fire. Not wanting to be delayed or further injured, the gang rode into the lake and managed to cross it by swimming their horses. Now even more soaked than before, they disappeared into the brush and the posse lost them.

Riding across cornfields to make better time, the gang came across a farmer and his team. They switched mounts and forced the farmer to show them the way through the woods, using the now-familiar ruse that they were a posse. They freed the farmer later that day and he went straight to the local law. He mentioned that one of the robbers, certainly Bob Younger, wore his arm in a sling and had blood on his sleeve. This man rode with one foot out of the stirrup, making the farmer believe that he had been injured in the leg as well.

The following day found the gang riding up a steep hill called "the Klondike." Perhaps they wanted to hide in a cave near the top, or maybe they wanted to see out over the surrounding countryside. The Klondike was the tallest hill in three counties. A posse spotted them and surrounded the hill. The slope was considered too steep for horses to descend so the neophyte lawmen figured they had the bandits trapped. After a long wait, some of their number went up the hill after nightfall and found the gang had managed to escape the trap.

That night the gang camped on a miserable little island in a swamp. Here they abandoned their horses. It's unclear why they decided to continue on foot. Cole Younger was hurt in the hip and Frank and Jesse James were both injured in the leg, so walking must surely have been excruciating. Perhaps the horses were simply too worn out to go on. They let the stolen ones loose and tied their own to trees. Once again their actions are unclear. If the object was to not have the horses traced, wouldn't it have been best to tie them all?

Sleeping out in the woods in the rain took its toll. Jim's shoulder wound and Bob's elbow wound both became infected. Bob developed a fever. Walking was hard business too. Some of the bandits' socks wore out and they had to make improvised ones cut from their underclothing. They ate hazel nuts, wild plums, and grapes, and what they could beg or steal from farms.

The next day, Sunday, September 10, Captain Rogers, who had clashed briefly with the outlaws already, telegraphed to all surrounding towns that he had the gang surrounded and called for reinforcements. Several posses obliged, as did cadets from Shattuck Academy and a regiment from Fort Snelling, which spread out in companies and combed the area. They found nothing.

The Northwestern Telegraph Company either helped or hindered the search by sending messages about the bandits for free. So many messages came in that the operator had to stay in his office around the clock, not getting any sleep and having to eat his meals at his telegraph key. The endless reports on the bandits scattered posses in all directions, chasing phantoms and rumors. Some of the sightings may have been of posses. Any group of armed strangers became suspect and several innocent men were arrested, causing a flurry of newspaper reports that the bandits had been captured, followed by shame-faced corrections. The confusion wasn't helped by the fact that two posses were led by active rivals – Minneapolis Detective Mike Hoy and St. Paul Detective John Brisette, who refused to cooperate or share information. Each wanted the glory all to himself.

Detective Brisette was the first to catch a glimpse of the fugitives when he and his 50 men chased them along the road west of Elysian township. He was joined in the hunt by Sheriff William Dill of Winona and 120 men, who spread out along the Winona & St. Peter Railroad hoping to spot the gang crossing the tracks. The rain had worsened, though, and the hoof prints were soon washed away. Many pickets guarding roads and bridges decided the weather wasn't worth fighting and left their posts.

It was now Monday, September 11. The rain didn't let up. The gang by this time had grown even more exhausted. In constant pain and weak from their wounds, eating what little they could scavenge or beg from farmers (thereby causing no end of telegraphic dispatches), they were becoming increasingly dispirited.

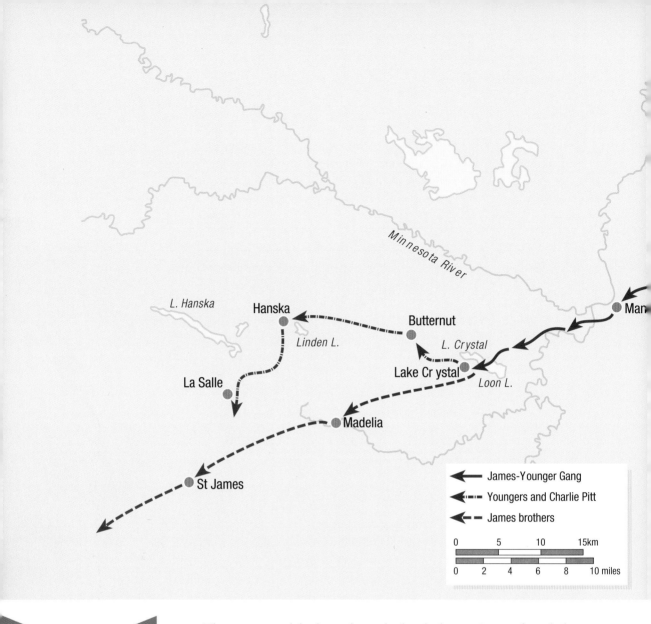

L. Hanska

Hanska

Linden L.

Butternut

L. Crystal

Lake Cr ystal

Loon L.

Minnesota River

Man

La Salle

Madelia

St James

James-Younger Gang

Youngers and Charlie Pitt

James brothers

| 0 | 5 | 10 | 15km |

| 0 | 2 | 4 | 6 | 8 | 10 miles |

SEPTEMBER 8

Gang has shootout
with a posse near
Tetonka Lake

The gang squelched on through the darkness. Dawn found them at Marysburg. They circled the town from a safe distance and discovered an abandoned farmhouse in the middle of some woods. This seemed like a good place to stop. They stayed there for the nights of September 11 and 12 to regain their strength. Even though they kept out of sight, reported sightings didn't stop and posses scurried around the area. The closest any came was one group who found the camp on the island. On Tuesday, September 12, a posse from Faribault found two of the gang's horses tied to a tree about five miles northwest of Lake Elysian and two or three miles south of German Lake. The animals were thoroughly worn out and so starved that they had nibbled away the bark. Five saddles lay nearby. In five days of flight, the gang had made it less than 50 miles from Northfield.

While some posses went home drenched and sick of the game, others took up the challenge. They may have been encouraged by the rising reward money. The $1,500 reward offer by Governor John Pillsbury was

a rich incentive, as was the $500 per head offered by the First National Bank of Northfield. The Winona & St. Peter Railroad offered an additional $700 and the Adams Express Company offered $1,000 per head. Picket lines were being set up all over the country. As the gang rested they were being hemmed in.

On Wednesday morning, September 13, the fugitives showed up at a farm and approached the farmhand, Jefferson Dunning. The bedraggled outlaws, on foot and in filthy, bloodstained clothes, pretended to be a posse but the ruse was a thin one. They demanded food and silence, or else. Dunning noted they were carrying bridles – none had been found with the saddles and horses – and this indicated the gang still hoped to find more horses. They finally admitted they were the robbers and tied Dunning's hands with a bridle and forced him to show them the way to Mankato, saying they needed to get across the Blue Earth River (a southern tributary of the Minnesota River) west of the town and asking if he thought they

SEPTEMBER 9

Gang rides up large hill named the Klondike and avoids a posse that tries to surround them

A drawing of two of the homes Jesse James lived in, including his childhood home and his last home. His local church is also shown. Much has been made in the James legend about Jesse's strict religion, including the anecdote that he always carried a heavily marked-up Bible. In reality, though, he broke several of the Ten Commandments and gave up his membership to the Baptist Church, saying he was unworthy. (LoC)

THE HOUSE IN WHICH JESSE JAMES ⟶ WAS KILLED.

THE HOME OF FRANK & JESSE JAMES

THE BAPTIST CHURCH KEARNEY MO. IN WHICH THE FUNERAL SERVICES WERE HELD.

could ford or swim across. Dunning said he thought they couldn't because the rain had swollen the river.

The gang asked Dunning if he knew where they were from and he replied that they were from Missouri. At this, one of the robbers grumbled, "We're a damned long way from Missouri." They also told him they wouldn't have shot Heywood if he had opened the safe and that on their next heist the cashier would be more cooperative.

At last the robbers stopped and debated whether they should let Dunning go or whether they should kill him to keep him silent. Dunning cried and begged for his life, insisting he wouldn't say a word. One outlaw was the most outspoken in favor of killing him, while another, whom Dunning later identified as Cole Younger, was adamant that he should be spared. At last the outlaw who wanted to kill him hauled Dunning over to where Bob Younger sat suffering from his badly wounded elbow and asked his opinion, adding that Dunning would get the entire countryside after them.

According to an interview Cole gave to the *Northfield News* on November 26, 1915, Bob replied, "I would rather be shot dead than to have that man killed for fear his telling might put a few hundred after us; there will be time enough for shooting if he should join in the pursuit."

Finally they let Dunning go after making him swear to keep his mouth shut. They also asked for his mailing address so they could "send him a handsome present." Dunning, of course, quickly spilled his tale. The story was relayed to the Mankato sheriff and the search was given new life. There is no record that Dunning ever received a present in the mail.

That evening a woman saw several strangers chasing around her chickens and stealing melons from her melon patch. Later they were spotted by Sheriff Davis of Faribault County on the Mankato–Good Thunder road. Having only one companion, Sheriff Davis wisely hid in the brush and watched them pass by, talking about horses. The gang then came to a bridge over the Blue Earth River at about 2am on the morning of Thursday, September 14. Several men guarded it, but the outlaws found the railroad bridge a quarter-mile away to be unguarded and they crossed there. General Pope had been told that railway employees would guard this bridge so he didn't send men there. The men the railroad posted spotted the bandits but were too scared to show themselves or even raise the alarm until the gang was well past. Some posses blundered through the countryside at night but saw nothing. Reinforcements from Mankato set out at dawn on Thursday.

Detective Hoy caught up with them at six on Thursday morning, September 14, when he and his men smelled a campfire at the bottom of a ravine near Minneopa Falls. Dismounting, the posse approached the camp and heard the fugitives running up the slope on the other side of the ravine. The gang left behind a bloodstained shirt and handkerchief, some roast chicken, corn, and one of their trademark overcoats.

Posse member Eric Olsen complained to the *Mankato Weekly Review* on September 26, "He [Detective Hoy] was in such a hurry to get off that he did not have time to hear. I told him to take it cool and lay his plans well before he started, but he rushed off with his men, and instead of following the trail, like on a deer hunt, carefully, and surround the fugitives, he let his men run a foot race past the robbers' camp, making a great noise, and when he discovered the camp the robbers had left. It is safe to say that Mr. Hoy's running so as to be the first to get the glory and reward, was the cause of the robbers' escape there."

When posse member Judson Jones, a man in ill-health, grumbled about Hoy's actions, the detective struck him. This didn't endear Hoy to the local population. In the end, Hoy's bumbling didn't matter, because a young boy's alertness would lead to the capture of some of the outlaws before they killed again.

Posses scoured all the area around the falls and, when it became apparent that the gang had slipped the noose yet again, set up pickets on all the roads, crossings, fords, and ferries to the west. General Pope changed his headquarters to the town of Lake Crystal to be close to the scene of the last sighting.

As the fugitives struggled through the Big Woods, the James brothers decided to leave the rest of the gang. They weren't as badly wounded as Bob and Jim Younger and could travel faster. Just what occurred during the conversation they had with their accomplices is a matter of controversy. Some accounts say the James brothers wanted to leave Bob behind or even that Jesse wanted to put him out of his misery but Cole Younger wouldn't hear of it. Others say the James brothers planned to act as a decoy to give the more wounded members of the gang a break. Why Pitts, who wasn't too badly injured, should stay with the slow-moving Younger brothers is a mystery. Perhaps their close friendship prevented him from leaving. In any case, on September 14 the James brothers set out on their own.

They stole a horse and, riding double, headed toward Lake Crystal and Loon Lake that evening. They got past one picket, and found another group of guards fast asleep. They might have made it if not for Richard Roberts,

W.I. SWAIN'S WESTERN SPECTACULAR PRODUCTION

JESSE JAMES.

"THIS MONEY BELONGS TO ME"

One of the innumerable stage productions of the Jesse James story. This play was performed in the 1880s. Plays and dime novels were turning the James brothers into legends while they were still at large committing crimes. (LoC)

SEPTEMBER 9, NIGHT

The gang sleeps on an island in a swamp and abandons their horses go

the only guard doing his job properly. Spotting the brothers, he fired at them and shot Jesse's hat off his head. The horse panicked and threw both of them into the mud. With the guards all waking up and making a clamor, the James brothers rushed off through a cornfield. Roberts later retrieved Jesse's hat, complete with bullet hole.

The "Jesse's hat" story is typical of the mythmaking around America's most famous outlaw. It could quite as easily have been Frank's hat. Roberts didn't know. Roberts told a newspaper that one man wore a bandage on his leg and that he shot the hat off the unbandaged man's head. He said that Frank had been wounded in the leg so he knew the other fellow had to be Jesse. It being nearly pitch dark, it's unclear how Roberts could have seen all this detail. Besides, both brothers had been wounded in the leg. But Jesse James was the more famous of the two so the local hero simply must have shot off Jesse's hat. This fame would one day lead to Jesse's death, while Frank would live to old age and die in his bed with his boots off.

Having outlaws loose in this rural area spooked the locals. As one old-timer remembered years later, "News at that time traveled slowly. No telephone, very few newspapers, so most of our information was spread by word of mouth, from house to house, etc. It was the wettest fall we ever experienced. All streams were swollen, bridges were out, the entire country was a quagmire… People were scared to death. They were afraid to leave homes during the day, and equally afraid to stay home during the night. Reports of all sorts were afloat."

TIONAL AND STARTLING "HOLD UP" OF THE "GOLD EXPRESS," BY FAMOUS WESTERN OUT

Frank and Jesse went to a farm and stole a team of horses at gunpoint. They cut up the harness to fashion reins and bridles, put sacks of hay on the animals' backs as saddles, and rode off. Pursuit wasn't far away and more than once the pair had to hide in the bushes while a posse passed within sight of them.

General Pope was still in command of the pursuit, as much as it was organized at all, and rode along with one of the posses. He sent the majority of his men after the James brothers, since they were the most recently sighted. Pope had realized the gang had split up but had no clear idea where the other four bandits might be.

The James brothers made good time and played the old ruse of being posse members. They called at farmhouses to get provisions and ask about roads and the location of other posses. For the most part the trick worked and they were soon getting ahead of the law. Frank even got his leg wound dressed, and the farmer who saw it said it was "only a flesh wound, and extended from near the hip on the outside of the leg, to near the knee, making an ugly gash or furrow."

Around noon on Saturday they crossed the Des Moines River at Swan's Ford. The recent sightings of the James brothers reinvigorated the manhunt. The *Sioux City Journal* for Sunday, September 17, reported, "Every person one meets on the cars along the St. Paul road is loaded down to the guards with fire-arms, resembling traveling arsenals. The greatest excitement prevails, and armed squads are moving to and fro continually. The hundreds

The Great Train Robbery, a lithograph from 1896, probably advertising a play. Outlaws were the renegade heroes of their day and their legend was firmly in place in the American consciousness long before movies and television helped bring it to later generations. (LoC)

SEPTEMBER 11 & 12

The gang rests at an abandoned farmhouse

Asle Oscar Sorbel, photographed at about the age he was when he spotted the fugitives from the bungled raid at Northfield. (Northfield Historical Society)

of men engaged in the chase appear to have no head or organized leaders, and consequently the chances of catching the fleeing ruffians are growing fainter and fainter each succeeding day."

After a brief respite the rain started up again, adding to the confusion and making life miserable for both pursuers and pursued. Frank and Jesse were spotted by a posse near Magnolia and some long-range shots were fired by both sides to no effect. A chase ensued but the James brothers got away. They abandoned their worn-out horses near Canton. There are many conflicting accounts at this point, and some of them say there were three robbers instead of two, one being seriously wounded and barely able to walk. Also, several reports from farmers tell of feeding the fugitives, and all remarked on their exhausted condition.

Northwest of Luverne, Sheriff Rice and three companions spotted them (on horseback again) but declined to shoot, fearing they'd be outfought. Instead the lawmen trailed them seven miles until darkness fell, when they were about three miles east of Palisade on Split Rock River. This marked the beginning of the Dakota Territory. Another posse discovered them at the river and exchanged a few shots with them. One of the outlaws grazed a posse member's mule in the neck, scaring off the pursuit.

Needing fresh mounts again, Frank and Jesse took two horses from Andrew Nelson that Sunday evening. One was blind in one eye and the other was blind in both eyes. After riding the horses for ten miles, they got rid of them and stole a better pair from a Mr. Burgeson five miles north of Sioux Falls. Someone galloped off to alert the authorities and one of the brothers shot his horse out from under him. News spread soon enough, however, and the James brothers hurried on their way.

Monday morning found them still close to Sioux Falls. They needed to cross the Missouri River but all the fords were guarded and a posse was only a few miles behind them. That night they rested at Ole Rongstad's place seven miles northeast of Canton. When they left, Rongstad and two others trailed them but fled when Rongstad's horse took a bullet in the neck. They had another close encounter with a posse and scared them off with a few shots.

On September 21, *The Sioux City Daily Journal* reported, "The sheriff from Worthington, who is here, seems to think that the robbers will make back tracks for the Sioux and strike out for the Jim River country. A large force is scattered over the prairies between Sioux and Rock rivers, and we are waiting anxiously for tidings from them. Had these men acted promptly they could have bagged their game this morning. . .The wounded man, who was with these two up to Sunday afternoon, has not been heard from since, and, as he was then scarcely able to stand, it is supposed that he probably died or has been left somewhere along the road."

This last statement is curious. It is not the only report to state that three outlaws were on the run in this district, although the majority states there were two. Some researchers have seen this as evidence of a ninth man at Northfield, a suggestion that is still debated by historians.

Tuesday, Wednesday, and Thursday (September 19–21) saw the trail growing colder, with locals seeing the bandits everywhere and posses seeing them nowhere. Lawmen, actual or self-proclaimed, descended on numerous innocent individuals, including an Indian couple snoozing in a vacant lot, a traveling laborer, and a cattle trader who had a suspicious wound in the leg that turned out to be several months old. When a whorehouse in Mankato was raided on the belief that the James brothers were hiding out there, the police didn't find them but did find two horse thieves they'd been looking for.

The trail disappeared. The James boys had escaped once again. For Pitts and the Youngers, however, the chase was heating up.

The four outlaws, wounded and losing strength, continued their weary trek through the forest. While Frank and Jesse had traveled 80 miles in the two days since they'd left, the rest of the gang had barely gone anywhere. They heard the shots taken at the James brothers near Lake Crystal and fled in the opposite direction. Their movements for a time are unclear, as they stayed well out of sight. Most posses had chased after Frank and Jesse, and so the rest of the gang had a brief respite.

September 21 found them still exhausted, and still in Minnesota. That morning they passed the farm of the Sorbel family and greeted the man of the house, Ole, who was working out front. Asle Oscar Sorbel, Ole's 16-year-old son, remembered that morning clearly. In a letter dated 1929 in the collection of Northfield expert John Koblas, Sorbel tells a friend:

> It was the 21st of September, just two weeks after the Raid. Mind you, it had been steady drizzling rain for two weeks and it was early morning. The sun was up about 20 minutes. We had the cattle in the road as it was too muddy in the pen. Jim Younger and Charley sic] Pitts came walking and they walked one on each side of pa. He was milking. I had come up to the gate, and as they were far enough so they did not hear me, I said to Pa, "That was the robbers." "No," he said, "they was nice men."
>
> I walked over to the road and their big toes showed in the mud. I said, "Come here. I will show you how nice men they are." He said, "You never mind. Go and milk." I milked one cow and then I set the pail inside the fence and started after them, but they crossed the creek about [80] yards west. I could see where they had gone into the timber. I went to three neighbors and told them.

The teenager ran up a hill but couldn't spot the strangers, so he instructed his neighbors to watch the roads from the hilltop while he returned to his family's farm to fetch a horse and ride to Madelia to alert the authorities. While he was running around the neighborhood, little did he know that two more robbers, one very weak and leaning on the other, walked up to his farm and asked his mother for some breakfast. They used their old line of being hunters and the good woman kindly offered to cook them something. They said they couldn't wait, paid for some bread and butter, and left. The boy grew even more excited when he came back and heard the news. In an interview with the September 26, 1876 edition of the *Mankato Weekly Review*, he said:

> I wanted to go to Ouren's [a neighbor] and tell them there were four. Father wouldn't let me – said they might shoot me. I sent one of my sisters over. Asked for a horse to go to town but he wouldn't let me have it. Then father said if I would go to the east road so they could not see me, he would let me have one. The horses were on the wagon, [I] unhitched them, took [the] harness off, took one and went through our fields and through one of the Torre Olson's, hollered to his folks that the robbers were around, went on to town. Ran him all I could.

Despite the muddy roads, Oscar made good time on the eight miles to Madelia. At one point the horse slipped and fell, tossing the boy face-first into the mud and leaving him covered from head to toe, but he got back in the saddle and kept pushing the animal as fast as it could go. Once in Madelia, the first person he informed was Colonel Thomas Vought, a local farmer and Union army veteran. Vought and county sheriff James Glispen organized a posse. It wasn't long before ten men had gathered at the Sorbel farm. As the news spread, other posses began to organize.

Sorbel's neighbors had been on the lookout from their workplaces and the tops of hills, and pointed the way to Sorbel and the posse. The bandits' trail entered some woods. To his enduring disappointment, the lad was left behind to hold the horses. Sheriff Glispen and his men finally caught up to the Younger brothers and Pitts at Hanska Slough, on the Watonwan River just south of Lake Hanska. The area was thick with underbrush and numerous small streams.

Seeing the outlaws walking along the slough, Sheriff Glispen called for them to halt. When they didn't, Glispen gave the order to fire, but the range was long and none of the bullets found their mark. The posse briefly lost sight of the fugitives in a thicket of willows and plum brush. The posse hurried along through the undergrowth and when they caught

Official CSA grave of Frank James, now preserved in the James Farm Museum. (Sean McLachlan)

SEPTEMBER 12

The gang's horses and island campsite are discovered

SEPTEMBER 13

Jefferson Dunning captured

Jesse James' original grave, picked apart by souvenir hunters and now preserved in the James Farm Museum. (Sean McLachlan)

SEPTEMBER 14, 6AM

Posse discovers gang's campsite at Minneopa Falls and forces them to flee

SEPTEMBER 14

The James brothers leave the rest of the gang to escape on their own

sight of them again they opened fire a second time. Cole Younger had been hobbling along with the aid of a walking stick he'd cut from a branch, and one of the bullets snapped it in two.

Across the river some distance away, a farmer was grazing his horses. The gang made for them, calling out, "We're lawmen and we're chasing bank robbers and we need you to bring your horses over the river to us." This ruse had now thoroughly worn out and the farmer chased his horses away. Then

The "Madelia Seven" who captured the Younger brothers and killed Charlie Pitts at Hanska Slough two weeks after the failed robbery at Northfield. This photograph, taken shortly after the shootout, shows them in front of the Flanders Hotel in Madelia. From left to right, they are: Sheriff James Glispen, Captain W.W. Murphy, George A. Bradford, Benjamin M. Rice, Colonel Thomas L. Vought, Charles A. Pomeroy, and S. James Severson. (Northfield Historical Society)

the gang turned towards a pair of men in the distance who had some horses, but the two brandished their shotguns and the gang continued to flee. Soon another posse led by Captain William Murphy, a seasoned veteran of the Union army, arrived on the scene just as fire from the gang made Glispen's party dismount and take cover.

The gang had trapped themselves. The high ground around the five acres of wooded slough was now watched on all sides except the south, where a sheer cliff forbade any escape. Cole Younger recalled that Charlie Pitts turned to him in despair and said, "We are entirely surrounded. We had better surrender."

"Charlie, this is where Cole Younger dies," Cole replied.

"All right, captain," Pitts replied. "I can die just as game as you can. Let's get it done."

The four outlaws readied their weapons and hid in a low settle behind a log, waiting for the attack they knew would come.

Sheriff Glispen turned to the 16 men with him and asked for volunteers to enter the slough. Only six, including Captain Murphy, volunteered.

The seven were a varied bunch. Sheriff James Glispen was serving his third term as sheriff of Watonwan County and was renowned for his physical fitness and his ability as a fist-fighter. William Murphy rose to the rank of Captain in the Union army during the Civil War, seeing hard fighting, a few bad wounds, and some time in Confederate prisons. Of the seven he had the most combat experience. Colonel Thomas Vought was another Civil War veteran. He owned the Flanders House hotel in Madelia, close to Hanska Slough, and had hosted some of the bandits on the night of August 23 when they were scouting the area for a "new railroad." After the shootout at Northfield, Vought remembered the wealthy travelers and knew they were part of the gang. George Bradford worked simultaneously as a farmer, clerk, schoolteacher, and shopkeeper and as far as is known had never heard a shot fired in anger. Neither had Benjamin Rice, but he had practiced until he was an expert marksman and his comrades noted that he was the "coolest in combat." Charles Pomeroy was another peaceful citizen who rose to the occasion without showing fear. S. James Severson was a clerk in a clothing store and one of the first to give chase when word came that the bandits were in the district.

They were a cross-section of Minnesota, a few seasoned veterans and some regular working Joes, and they had volunteered to fight the most notorious gunmen of their day. They gathered around for a final conference.

"Here's the way we'll do it then," Glispen said. "Form a line 15 feet apart, and we'll walk right at 'em. When we see 'em, demand their surrender. If they shoot, shoot them. Shoot to kill, and keep on shooting until they surrender or are all dead, or we are!"

Another variant of the story relates that these words belonged to Captain Murphy, whom Glispen had put in charge because of his war experience.

The men spread out in a skirmish line 15ft apart. They agreed to shoot low in the hope of wounding the outlaws and capturing them alive. As they crept along through the underbrush, climbing over fallen trees and ducking under vines, suddenly Charlie Pitts jumped into view and fired. Glispen dropped to one knee and shot him in the chest. Pitts fell as the rest of the posse opened up on him. They needn't have bothered; Glispen had shot him straight through the heart.

The outlaws started a tremendous fusillade and didn't let up. As posse member George Bradford recalled, "I had raised my gun to shoot, when a bullet struck, or rather grazed, my wrist and disturbed my aim, so it was a second or so before I fired. Several shots were fired from both sides and a volley from across the river, from parties there. They could not see us from there, but fired, the bullets cutting the twigs over our heads."

Colonel Thomas Vought felt a sharp blow just above the waist and thought he'd taken a gut shot. He was surprised to not see any blood, and then he realized the bullet had smashed a large rosewood pipe in his lower vest pocket, not piercing his flesh at all.

Cole Younger realized they had to break out and he rose up to start a charge. "The next thing I knew," he writes in his memoirs, "I was lying on the ground, bleeding from my nose and mouth."

Jim was the next to fall, a rifle bullet passing through the front of his upper jaw and taking out all the teeth on his left side. This knocked him out. Cole got shot above the right eye. While the bullet didn't pierce his skull, it did knock him unconscious.

For a moment all was silent. Bob Younger called out, "I surrender. They're all down but me."

Sheriff Glispen ordered his men to hold their fire and Bob appeared with a white handkerchief raised above his head in his one good hand. As he came out of the low settle in which the robbers had hidden, one of the men standing across the river shot him. The bullet grazed his good arm and the nearly unconscious bandit fell down.

Bob's weak voice came through the brush, "I was surrendering. Someone shot me while I was surrendering."

Captain Murphy bellowed at the men, who hadn't been brave enough to get close to the action, that the robbers had surrendered and to stop firing.

The posse went over to Bob and helped him up. They next approached Cole Younger, who was just coming to. Being peppered full of bullets hadn't dampened his spirits. Oscar Sorbel told the October 16, 1924 edition of the *St. James Plain Dealer* that, "Cole Younger had one bullet and some buckshot received at Northfield, besides ten fresh buckshot in his body, but he did not pray. He offered to fight two of our best men at once. He said he had been dogged for two weeks in the rain, with nothing to eat, but he could lick two of our best men. Bob slung his left arm around him and said, 'Come, or we will be hanged.' But Cole said he did not care, and that he would just as soon hang today as tomorrow."

Some of the onlookers shouted that the gang should be lynched, but those who had actually done the fighting told them off.

The outlaws were put on a wagon and driven to the nearby town of Madelia as Jim Younger hung over the side drooling blood from his shattered mouth. A crowd of curiosity seekers followed. Some applauded the outlaws for putting up such a good fight and Cole Younger managed to stagger to his feet and tip his hat to his admirers. The three brothers were given medical attention and it was found that Cole had suffered 11 bullet wounds. The doctor removed Manning's bullet from the Cole's hip and returned it to its owner. Manning started carrying it around as a good-luck charm. Jim had taken five hits. Besides the elbow shattered at Northfield, Bob Younger had a nick to the arm and a bullet lodged in his chest from the gunfight at Hanska Slough. All were exhausted. People dressed their wounds and fed them. One local woman even sent flowers. They were offered clean clothing and when Cole took his boots off, the nails of his big toes came off with them.

The captured men soon began to talk and recounted their flight through the woods. Cole Younger said that Pitts was the man who shot Heywood, but that may have been a way to avoid culpability for any gang member still living. In later years he hinted that Frank James did the deed and most historians believe this to be correct. Cole also claimed Heywood was shot because he was going for a gun, although this has long been disputed since in fact the gun at the counter had already been taken during the hold-up and contemporary reports did not mention a second weapon in the bank. Once again it seems a case of a criminal trying to justify unjustifiable actions. The brothers were transferred to the jail at nearby Faribault. Rumors of a rescue attempt by the gang were rife and the jail was heavily guarded.

When asked who the other two bandits were, they said their names were Woodson and Howard and that they were new members of the gang and not well known to the Younger brothers. Woodson and Howard were later

SAMUEL WELLS, ALIAS CHARLIE PITTS (UNKNOWN–SEPTEMBER 21, 1876)

Very little is known for certain about this gang member. So little, in fact, that he is better known by his alias than his real name.

Accounts say Wells/Pitts was foul-tempered, nearly always scowling, and deadly. Otterville train robber Hobbs Kerry said of him, "Pitts is the one summoned when 'dirty work' is on hand." In his memoirs, Cole Younger spoke of his bravery and willingness to die rather than be captured. Although these reports make Wells/Pitts appear as a seasoned outlaw, there is little evidence of crimes other than the Otterville and Northfield robberies.

Wells/Pitts was a neighbor of the Younger family at Lee's Summit, Missouri, and was the one who discovered the Younger brothers' father after he had been murdered by Union soldiers in 1862. Wells/Pitts used his familiarity with the family to get into the gang. He was said to be an expert with horses and valued by his fellows for his skill at picking the best steeds to buy or steal and for his ability to care for them.

Wells/Pitts died in the shootout in Hanska Slough. His body ended up in the possession of Dr. Frank Murphy, surgeon general of Minnesota. The dead bandit was put on display for a time and Murphy later gave the remains to Dr. Henry Hoyt, who sank them in Lake Como outside St. Paul so they could decompose. They were found and a murder investigation was launched until Hoyt cleared up the matter.

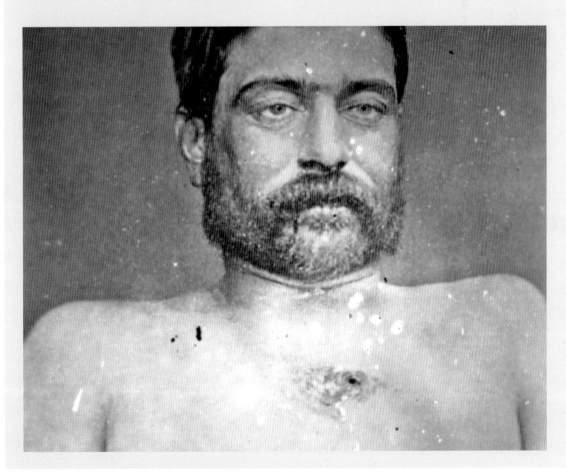

Charlie Pitts after being killed at Hanska Slough. (Northfield Historical Society)

Jesse James after he had been shot by Robert Ford in 1882. He has a full beard and looks much as he would have during the Northfield raid. Death photography was highly popular in 19th-century America, not just for famous murder victims and dead outlaws but for common people as well. (LoC)

proven to be aliases used by Frank and Jesse. Once on the cart leading away from their last stand, Cole had let slip the question, "Did Frank and Jesse escape?" but now that he had his wits about him, he kept their identities secret. This and the general knowledge that the Younger brothers rode with the James brothers from time to time made most people assume Frank and Jesse were the two who had escaped. Faribault sheriff Ara Barton tried to coax the names out of them, hinting that the courts would go easier on them if they talked. Barton gave Cole a piece of paper to write the names down, and Cole wrote, "Be true to your friends if the heavens fall. Cole Younger."

The throngs of visitors and the media circus led to one final tragedy in the Northfield saga. On October 2 at four o'clock in the morning, one of the guards doing sentry duty outside the Faribault jail, Frank Glazier, saw a man enter the yard. Glazier ordered him to halt and asked, "Who are you?" The man replied, "Don't you know me? I am the city police," while moving his hand to his chest and continuing to advance. Glazier thought he was going for a gun and shot him dead.

The stranger had spoken the truth. He was William Kapanick of the night watch. It's not known why Kapanick failed to stop and identify himself. An inquest cleared Glazier.

With the majority of the robbers dead or behind bars, attention turned to the widow and daughter of cashier Joseph Lee Heywood. He was lauded as a hero for not opening the safe and his employers circulated a letter to banks across the U.S. and Canada to raise a fund for his family's care. More than $30,000 was collected, a large sum at that time.

A long and unseemly battle erupted over the reward money, with claims and counterclaims shooting back and forth as thick and vicious as the bullets at Hanska Slough. When the smoke cleared, the seven posse members and Oscar Sorbel received equal parts of the state reward money, $46.25 each, plus $200 each from the bank, meaning each got $246.25. Another 35 men received a share of state money and $10 from the bank, totaling $56.25 each. Another 15 men who hung back even more than these 35 half-heroes got $8 each.

Cole, Jim, and Bob all pleaded guilty on November 18, which in Minnesota at that time kept them safe from being given the death penalty. Instead, they were sentenced to life in prison and they were sent to Stillwater Penitentiary. Bob Younger died of consumption behind bars in 1889. Jim and Cole acted as model prisoners and after serving 25 years were released in 1901. Jim had trouble adjusting to life outside and after losing his job due to an injury and being forbidden by the terms of his parole to marry he took his own life. He had been out of jail for only three months.

Cole fared better. At first life was hard and he worked a number of jobs, including the ironic position of traveling tombstone salesman. He soon turned to public life, authoring his myth-laden autobiography *The Story of Cole Younger by Himself*, and running a Wild West show with Frank James, who had since turned himself in and had been cleared of all crimes. After the show went bust, Younger went on the speaking circuit with a lecture about why crime doesn't pay. He died in 1916, long after most of the major figures of the Wild West had passed on. Many dubbed him "the last of the great outlaws."

And Frank and Jesse? They got away and laid low for a time in Tennessee under the names Woodson and Howard. The Northfield fiasco seriously

Last Stand of the Younger Brothers (overleaf)
On September 21, 1876, two weeks after the Northfield raid, the Younger brothers and Charlie Pitts were finally run to ground by a posse of seven men. The gang made their stand in Hanska Slough. Other posses and onlookers were nearby and the gang was surrounded. Pitts was shot through the heart at the beginning of the fight and Jim Younger was soon shot through the mouth, knocking him out. As this was happening, Cole Younger rose from the gang's position behind a log and decided to make a break for it, guns blazing. He was quickly knocked out by a bullet ricocheting off his skull above the right eye. Bob Younger, severely weakened by wounds received at Northfield, kept up a steady fire until he was the only one left conscious. At this point he surrendered. Three posse members were slightly injured.

rattled Frank, and he decided to go straight. Jesse heard the call of the trail, however, and assembled a gang in late 1879 to rob the train at Glendale, Missouri. Frank soon got pulled back in.

ANALYSIS

A hard look at the Northfield raid takes much of the shine off the myth of the James–Younger gang. The bandits committed numerous basic mistakes that were inexplicable coming from such experienced outlaws and former bushwhackers.

Their choice of Minnesota was both a good and a bad one. The James and Younger brothers had committed too many robberies in their home state of Missouri and lawmen of all stripes were out in force searching for them. While the Otterville train robbery went well, they couldn't expect to get away with robbing so close to home forever and picking a distant target made sense. The gang had already hit targets in other states and with Bill Stiles along as a guide, they stood a good chance of pulling it off. Having some of the gang ride with Stiles to Minnesota was a wise move in order to familiarize more of the robbers with the area. They invested in maps and asked numerous questions along the way. Even when desperately hunted, the gang was never completely lost.

The mistakes began when they got to Minnesota. Several members pulled various stunts that got them noticed, a bad move for famous outlaws preparing a heist. None of this ended up mattering, however, and Northfield was taken completely by surprise. What should have been a robbery as easy as all the rest turned bad for several reasons. First, they had severely underestimated the Minnesotans' will to fight. The gang cannot really be blamed for this, because this was the most resistance they had encountered in any of their jobs. Just why the citizens of Northfield rose up in rage when the inhabitants of so many other towns hid away is a matter of conjecture. Part of the reason may be that the gang's fame preceded them, that any town with a bank was on the knife's edge, nervous about a robbery. The timing of the hunting season and the large crowd downtown that day didn't help either.

Besides the plucky crowd, most of the problems were of the robbers' own making. Some hit the bottle before the robbery. Cole Younger later said that if he had known some of his accomplices were drunk, he would have

ROBERT EWING "BOB" YOUNGER (OCTOBER 29, 1853– SEPTEMBER 16, 1889)

The youngest of the outlaw Youngers, Bob didn't serve in the Civil War and was desperate to prove himself. He may have participated in the gang's Adair, Iowa, train robbery in 1873 in what was perhaps his first crime. He was certainly present at Otterville, although after his capture at Hanska Slough he told reporter John Jay Lemon that he "was a novice and had only been in a few scrapes."

Described as good-looking, soft-spoken, and likeable, he felt remorse at having pressured his brothers to join the Northfield raid. Bob was sentenced to life in prison and was incarcerated in Stillwater Prison with his brothers. In 1898, Bob's brother Jim Younger wrote to a friend from prison:

"The one time Bob listened to outside influences, firmly insisting that he was a man and could lead his own life, resulted in the Northfield affair. He was led to believe the subtly drawn picture by that master artist, the crafty Mephistopheles, Jesse James, that there was a way of quick revenge on the North for our father's financial losses and the recovery of a huge sum of money. I never saw him so blindly enthused. Neither Cole or I could reach him ... Bob asked so many times if we forgave him for being so headstrong, both Cole and I assured him we were more at fault, being older, we should have found a way to prevent the whole thing."

Bob Younger died of consumption while still behind bars.

Bob Younger, the youngest of the Younger brothers and the most eager to rob a bank in Minnesota. This picture was taken shortly after his capture at Hanska Slough. All three Younger brothers were fed, clothed, and had their wounds tended to before having their photos taken. (Northfield Historical Society)

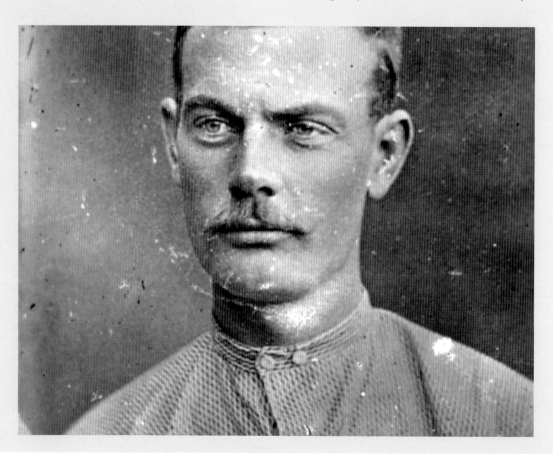

JAMES HARDIN "JIM" YOUNGER (JANUARY 15, 1848–OCTOBER 19, 1902)

Born on Cole's birthday four years after his older brother, Jim Younger also rode with Quantrill, joining in 1864. He was captured in Kentucky in 1865 after a skirmish that left Quantrill mortally wounded and several other guerrillas dead or captured. He and a few of the other prisoners soon escaped.

Jim was a latecomer to the James–Younger gang. In fact, he served as a deputy sheriff of Dallas County, Texas, from 1870 to 1871. Quieter and more thoughtful than his big brother Cole, he often deferred to him and ended up joining the gang sometime in the mid-1870s. He may have been involved in the gang's 1873 robbery of a train in Adair, Iowa, and certainly participated in the March 16, 1874 shootout that left a Pinkerton agent and the agent's guide dead. Jim tried to go straight, but was once again pulled into the gang to participate in the Northfield heist. When his sister Retta visited him shortly after his capture at Hanska Slough, she cried, "Oh! Jim, this is too bad. If it had not been for Cole and Bob you would never have been here. They enticed you to do this." Reporter John Jay Lemon said she acted coolly to the other two brothers, only deigning to shake their hands.

Jim served in Stillwater Prison with his brothers and was released on the same day as Cole. By that time he had wasted away physically and was severely depressed. While in prison he met female reporter Alix Mueller. During his incarceration Jim had become a socialist and an advocate of women's rights, and became interested in this assertive woman who worked in a profession unusual for her sex. The couple fell in love and became engaged upon his release in 1901. The terms of his parole kept him from getting married. Alix's parents didn't like Jim's notorious past and convinced their daughter to move to Idaho. Jim's parole dictated that he couldn't leave Minnesota. Despondent over the possibility of never seeing her again, Jim Younger committed suicide in St. Paul.

Jim Younger after his capture at Hanska Slough. The painful and debilitating mouth wound he received in that firefight can clearly be seen. His inability to eat solid food ruined his health and contributed to the severe depression that eventually led him to take his own life. (Northfield Historical Society)

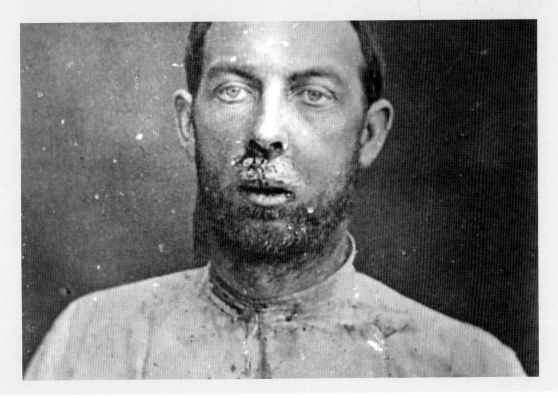

An elderly Frank James selling tickets to visit the family home. In earlier years it was his mother who sold the tickets. Zerelda James/Samuels would also sell pebbles from Jesse's grave at 25 cents apiece. When she ran out of pebbles, she would go down to a nearby stream and collect more. The James Farm Museum still sells pebbles, and they still cost 25 cents. (Missouri State Archives)

Last Picture of Frank James, "The Outlaw" taken at his farm near Excelsior Springs, Mo.

never ridden into Northfield that day. That seems like more of his later garlanding of the facts, however. The drunken members of the gang probably reunited with the rest before the robbery (although Cole denies this) so Cole would have had a chance to back out then. Perhaps he felt, as he had in Missouri, that he owed it to his younger brother Bob to see him through safely. Still, he could have been more adamant that the robbery be called off for another day.

The gang also made a mistake in robbing a bank when there were so many people on the street, but since Northfield was a busy town with a compact business center, this could not have been avoided if the gang insisted on hitting Northfield. The town's second bank, right around the corner, faced Mill Square and was equally central.

The gang also didn't cut the telegraph wires. On bushwhacker raids during the war and earlier heists, this was usually done before or right after the raid. Cole later said that they planned to cut the wires after the robbery and the gunfight didn't give them the chance, but given the size of the town they should have done it beforehand. This major blunder allowed news of the robbery and the gang's movements to be broadcast across the state, and effective pursuit was organized far earlier than it otherwise would have been.

The gang's actions became increasingly erratic as they fled Northfield. Their bumbling with the posse at Shieldsville – not taking their guns and shooting up the town pump – showed their state of mind at the time. They were wounded and in shock at the resistance they'd met. In their bushwhacker

Frank James later in life after he'd gone straight. Frank lived a peaceful life but, like his old partner in crime Cole Younger, wasn't adverse to publicity. He gave tours of the James farm and numerous interviews with the press. (LoC)

SEPTEMBER 18

James brothers have two shootouts but escape unharmed

SEPTEMBER 21

The Younger brothers and Pitts are recognized by Asle Oscar Sorbel, who gives the alarm. The gang is cornered in Hanska Slough. Pitts is killed and the Youngers surrender

NOVEMBER 18

The Younger brothers plead guilty in order to escape the death penalty

days they would have disappeared into the woods and found one of their many hideouts. But it wasn't their bushwhacker days; they were far from their familiar Missouri haunts and their only local expert lay dead in the street. It appears the gang panicked. This was unusual because most were experienced fighters who had suffered reverses before. Perhaps their life of crime had been too easy until this point. The alcohol didn't help either.

It wasn't long before the outlaws got their senses back. Soon they were trying to hide their tracks, passing across streams and through the thick woods. They even slogged through a swamp for a time, although this might be evidence that they were in fact lost. Still, reports of their passing were regularly relayed to the authorities. The gang had not packed any provisions so they were forced to stop at farmhouses to buy, beg, or steal food. The countryside was on the alert and every stop led to more reports. With the populace so excited, however, there were plenty of false sightings, and only this and the disorganization of the manhunt kept the gang from being captured earlier.

Frank and Jesse James made the right decision when they decided to split with the gang. They drew off much of the pursuit and gave the Younger brothers and Pitts time to rest and recover. The James brothers were probably acting selfishly, pretending to help while really just wanting to get away from the slower members of the gang. Whatever their motives, their help did little to change the outcome. The Younger brothers and Pitts didn't take advantage of their respite to hurry out of the region. Instead they went into hiding. This gave them some much-needed rest but they were too wounded to fully recover in such a short time. Once they started running again, their energy soon wore out.

Considering the disorganization of the pursuit, with a little more planning and foresight the gang should have gotten away even with their injuries. There was no FBI or National Guard at the time; law enforcement was the responsibility of a patchwork of different agencies, including local sheriffs, Pinkerton agents, and detectives from nearby cities. Posses of civilians often hunted criminals, and the large rewards offered for the James–Younger gang encouraged every farmer to grab his shotgun, saddle up his plough horse, and join the hunt. Despite General Pope's best efforts, these groups remained under separate commands, or no command at all, while competing big-city detectives vied with one another to bag the big prize. In the end it took the clear thinking of a teenager and the bravery of seven men who until that moment hadn't even glimpsed the bandits to capture the Younger brothers and kill Pitts.

CONCLUSION

For the first time in their history, the towns of Northfield and Madelia were on the map. Neither town has forgotten the events of those weeks. Madelia has a reenactment every September of the gunfight in Hanska Slough. Every year on the weekend after Labor Day, Northfield celebrates the raid with the Defeat of Jesse James Days. The event has been held since 1948. Of course, there was a large celebration after the gang was defeated, with much carousing in the streets and the setting off of "anvil artillery." This odd custom involved igniting a keg of gunpowder under an anvil and shooting it high into the air. Sadly, modern safety standards (and plain good sense) have kept this great American tradition from being continued in the present day.

The James gang was never the same after the Northfield raid. With many of the old comrades dead or behind bars, the new gang members weren't of the same quality. After a few jobs with the new outfit, Frank drifted away from his increasingly erratic brother and gave up his life of crime for good. Jesse moved from place to place, committing more robberies and gathering around him aspiring bandits and shifty characters like Robert Ford, who eventually shot the famous outlaw in the back at Jesse's family home on April 3, 1882.

Frank got in touch with the Missouri governor and made terms for his surrender. He was tried and found not guilty of all charges. This may have been part of the deal. It also helped that so many witnesses were dead. He and Cole ran a Wild West show for a time before slipping into quieter pursuits. Both seem to have made an earnest effort to go straight, and after Frank's surrender and Cole's release, there is no evidence that they ever broke any law.

Perhaps they felt the years weighing down. Perhaps they were simply too tired. Shortly after he surrendered, Frank James gave an interview to the *St. Louis Republican* on October 6, 1882 in which he described the life of the outlaw as "…a life of taut nerves, of night-riding and day-hiding, of constant listening for footfalls, crackling twigs, rustling leaves and creaking doors … of seeing Judas in the face of every friend."

A bandit entertains the crowd at Northfield's annual "Defeat of Jesse James Days." (Northfield Historical Society)

BIBLIOGRAPHY

Beights, Ronald, *Jesse James and the First Missouri Train Robbery*, Gretna, LA: Pelican Publishing (2002)

Brant, Marley, *The Outlaw Youngers: A Confederate Brotherhood*, Lanham, MD: Madison Books (1995)

Brownlee, Richard S., *Gray Ghosts of the Confederacy: Guerilla Warfare in the West, 1861–1865*, Baton Rouge, LA: Louisiana State University Press (1984)

Christensen, Lawrence, et al., *Dictionary of Missouri Biography*, Columbia, MO: University of Missouri Press (1999)

Christensen, Lawrence, and Kremer, Gary, Kremer. *A History of Missouri. Volume IV: 1875 to 1919*, Columbia, MO: University of Missouri Press (1973)

Croy, Homer, *Last of the Great Outlaws: The Story of Cole Younger*, New York: Duell, Sloan and Pearce (1956)

Edwards, John Newman, *A Terrible Quintette*, London: Hurstwood Enterprises Ltd (2002)

Gilles, Albert S., "Jesse, Frank, and Cole," *Frontier Times* (September 1969)

James Jr., Jesse, *Jesse James, My Father*, New York City, NY: Frederick Fell (1957)

Koblas, John, *Faithful unto Death: The James–Younger Raid on the First National Bank, Northfield, Minnesota, September 7, 1876*, Northfield, MN: Northfield Historical Society (2001)

Koblas, John, *Jesse James Northfield Raid: Confessions of the Ninth Man*, St. Cloud, MN: North Star Press (1999)

Lemon, John Jay, *The Northfield Tragedy*, St. Paul, MN: Privately published 1876; Reprinted in London by Westerners Publications Ltd (2001)

Leslie, Edward, *The Devil Knows How to Ride: The True Story of William Clarke Quantrill and His Confederate Raiders*, New York, NY: Da Capo Press (1996)

McCorkle, John, *Three Years with Quantrill*, Norman, OK: University of Oklahoma Press (1992)

Parrish, William, *A History of Missouri, Volume III: 1860 to 1875*, Columbia, MO: University of Missouri Press, (1973).

McLachlan, Sean, *American Civil War Guerrilla Tactics*, Oxford: Osprey Publishing (2009)

McLachlan, Sean, *It Happened in Missouri*, Guilford, CT: Globe Pequot Press (2008)

Robinson III, Charles M., *American Frontier Lawmen 1850–1930*, Oxford: Osprey Publishing (2005)

Settle, William A., *Jesse James Was His Name*, Columbia, MO: University of Missouri Press (1966)

Steele, Philip W. and Warfel, George, *The Many Faces of Jesse James*,

The First National Bank has retained its original façade, making it a good backdrop for reenactors. (Northfield Historical Society)

Gretna, LA: Pelican Publishing (1998)

U.S. War Department, *The War of the Rebellion: A Compilation of the Official Records of the Union and Confederate Armies*, Washington, DC: Government Printing Office (1888)

Various authors, *Caught in the Storm: A Field Guide to the James & Younger Gang Escape Trail*, Northfield, MN: Northfield Historical Society (2008)

Wood, Larry, *Ozarks Gunfights and other Notorious Incidents*, Gretna, LA : Pelican Publishing2010).

Yeatman, Ted, *Frank and Jesse James: The Story Behind the Legend*, Nashville, TN: Cumberland House (2000)

Younger, Cole, *The Story of Cole Younger by Himself*, St. Paul, MN: Minnesota Historical Society Press (2000)

INDEX